# The Scout Troop

## A handbook for Scout Leaders and Patrol Leaders


*Written by*

**Ron Jeffries and Paul Moynihan**

*Illustrated by*

**Peter Harrison**

*Designed by*

**Bill Bruce**



Scouts

The Scout Association, Baden-Powell House,
Queen's Gate, LONDON SW7 5JS

# About this book

This book has been planned to help both Scout Leaders and Patrol Leaders. The **Chapters** contain information and ideas to assist leaders in implementing the Scout Section Training Programme and on leadership, programme planning and administration. The **Action** pages (which are spread throughout the book) have suggestions for programmes and activities. There is a **Reference** section at the end of the book.

Throughout the text reference is made to the Scout County; in Scotland the equivalent is the Scout Area.



ISBN 0 85165 186 0

First Edition
April 1985

Printed in Great Britain by Eyre and Spottiswoode
Ltd at Grosvenor Press, Portsmouth.

# The Scout Troop

## Contents

Chapter 1

# So now you are a leader . . .

This book is for all leaders in the Scout Troop – for Patrol Leaders and for Scouters.

Have you ever asked yourself why you came into the Scouts? There must be as many answers as there are Patrol Leaders and Scouters. Perhaps the activities attracted you? Was it the chance to try something new or to get involved in your local community?

Whatever your reasons, the other Scouts and leaders in the Troop joined for similar things, too. Like you, they want to enjoy their Scouting and to feel a part of what's going on.

It's your job as a leader to help your Scouts to do just that. If you are going to offer activities that will hold their interest, you will need to know what your Scouts enjoy doing, what their hobbies are and what they are good at. By getting to know your Scouts in this way, you will be able to offer a challenging and exciting programme.

The Scout Patrol is a small group of six to eight friends, led by a Patrol Leader who has an Assistant Patrol Leader. Patrols form a Scout Troop, led by a Scout Leader, who will have Assistant Scout Leaders and others to help him.

The Patrols will have activities on their own and come together as a Troop. From time to time small groups of Scouts (of similar or different ages) will work on a common interest or project. Individual Scouts, Patrols, Troops, Patrol Leaders and Scouters will meet for activities and training with others in the District, in the County and beyond. The Patrol and Troop do not exist by themselves – they are part (and an important part) of something bigger . . .

## The Scout Group

A Cub Scout Pack, a Scout Troop and a Venture Scout Unit together form a Scout Group, under the guidance of a Group Scout Leader. There may be more than one Pack or Troop and many Scout Groups have Beaver Colonies.

Beavers are boys aged 6 and 7, formed into a Beaver Colony with adults as Beaver Leaders and Assistant Beaver Leaders.

A Cub Scout Pack is for 8 to 10½ year-olds in Sixes (with a Sixer and Second), led by a Cub Scout Leader who works with Assistant Cub Scout Leaders and Instructors. The Sixers meet with the Leaders as a Sixers' Council to plan activities for the Pack.

Venture Scouts are young men and women of 15½ to 20, planning their own programme through an elected Unit Executive Committee, with a Venture Scout Leader, Assistant Venture Scout Leaders and other specialists offering backing and support.

The Scout Troop is central to the life of the Scout Group, catering for the 10½ to 15½-year-olds, working in Patrols and through the Patrol Leaders' Council (both of which will be explored later).

There is flexibility in the age at which a Cub Scout moves to the Troop (between 10 and 11) and when a Scout goes into the Unit (15 to 16). Much depends on the youngster's development and his

## Aim and Method

The Aim of The Scout Association is to encourage the physical, mental and spiritual development of young people so that they may take a constructive place in society.

The Method of achieving the Aim of the Association is by providing an enjoyable and attractive scheme of progressive training, based on the Scout Promise and Law and guided by adult leadership.

personal circumstances, for the transition needs to be smooth and it is often best if the move is made with a group of friends.

Regular discussion on this and other topics between the Scouters in the Sections of the Group takes place at the Group Scouters' Meeting, attended by all Leaders, Assistant Leaders and the Chairman of the Venture Scout Unit Executive Committee, and chaired by the Group Scout Leader. The Scout Section's Leaders will want to bring forward the views expressed at the Patrol Leaders' Council to this meeting.

The Group Council is the supporting body of the Scout Group. All Leaders, Assistant Leaders, Instructors (including Cub Scout Instructors), Patrol Leaders and Venture Scouts are members of the Group Council, together with the Sponsoring Authority (if there is one), Administrators, Advisers, parents and supporters of the Group.

An Annual General Meeting is held once a year at which the Group Council elects some of its members to the Group Executive Committee, which is responsible for the day to day running of the Group. The Group Scout Leader, the Scout Leader and other Section Leaders are members of the Group Executive Committee, which is chaired by the Group Chairman.

The Sections provide a progressive training programme, which is co-ordinated and supported within the Scout Group, so that the Pack, the Troop and the Unit are not working in isolation and apart from each other (and this is discussed further in Chapter 5). Members of the Group Council will help with fund raising, with the maintenance of equipment and premises and in many other ways – leaving the Scouters to concentrate on their prime task of working with young people.

## The Scout Promise

On my honour, I promise that I will
do my best to do my duty to God
and to the Queen,
to help other people
and to keep the Scout Law.

# The Scout District

Others are ready to help you to improve the quality of the programme you offer to the Patrol and Troop (through training days, courses and the like) and to widen the scope of activities (by making available equipment and expertise). We repeat – you are not alone!

There is the Scout District, which is made up of all the Scout Groups within your locality and led by the District Commissioner and his team of Assistant District Commissioners. The District Scout Council and the District Executive Committee have similar functions to their opposite numbers in the Group, although their make-up is different. They provide their support with

## The Scout Law

1. A Scout is to be trusted.
2. A Scout is loyal.
3. A Scout is friendly and considerate.
4. A Scout is a brother to all Scouts.
5. A Scout has courage in all difficulties.
6. A Scout makes good use of his time and is careful of possessions and property.
7. A Scout has respect for himself and for others.

premises and camp sites, fund raising and so on. The District Scout Fellowship offers valuable back-up support in this and other ways.

District Scouters' Meetings bring Scout Leaders and Assistant Scout Leaders together for training and to plan activities – activities that it might be difficult for a Troop to run on its own, such as Proficiency Badge courses, specialist pursuits and the like. Sometimes Patrol Leaders will be invited to attend District Scouters' Meetings.

From time to time a District Patrol Leader's Council may be formed. All Patrol Leaders (or, perhaps, one or two from each Troop) meet together under the chairmanship of an experienced Patrol Leader to exchange views and to plan activities. The Assistant District Commissioner (Scouts) and one or two Scouters may be present, but it is best not to have too many adult leaders around so that the Patrol Leaders do not feel inhibited in their discussions. This will also encourage them to make decisions themselves.

# And beyond . . .

The Scout County, led by the County Commissioner with a team of Assistant County Commissioners, offers training courses and practical help. Specialists in water and air activities, in working with the handicapped and in a range of adventurous pursuits will be available. County gatherings and expeditions will give your Scouts the chance to take part in a wider range of activities and enable them to meet Scouts from other areas.

There is support, too, in your local community – amongst the religious bodies, industry, commerce, ethnic groups and other organisations concerned with young people and education. Scouting, as part of the youth service, is involved in local youth committees – both to receive help and to support other member organisations. Nationally, the Scouts are active members of the British Youth Council and the National Council for Voluntary Youth Services and work closely with like-minded bodies.

The Chief Scout heads the Movement in the United Kingdom and has a team of Headquarters Commissioners. The Headquarters Commissioner for Scouts, working with the National Scout Advisory Board, is concerned with all matters affecting the Scout Section, its programme and development, and the training of its leaders.

# Enjoy

Enjoying what you are doing as a leader in the Scouts is important.

Don't be too ambitious at the start. Take your time and confidence in planning – and seeing an activity through – will grow with experience. Try not to do everything yourself: involve others, letting them feel that their part is valued and appreciated.

## Action 1

Here are some activities to get started. Try them at Patrol meetings and then adapt them for the larger numbers on Troop Night. Most require little in the way of equipment.

# Observation

**On the line**

Attach 20 objects to a rope stretched across the room. Give the Scouts one minute to look at the objects and then take the rope outside. Replace a third of the objects with others and give the Patrol another minute to note the changes. Take the rope away again and ask each Scout to write out a list of the 20 objects they were shown first and those that were substituted.

**How many?**

Make a collection of nails, screws, buttons, drawing pins and keys of different shapes and sizes. Show the items to the Patrol for a minute and then cover them up. Prepare a series of questions and give each Scout a pencil and paper to write down his answers – how many one inch nails, blue buttons, brass screws, green drawing pins etc.?

**Sound effects**

Fix a screen behind which the Assistant Patrol Leader acts out a number of sound effects – eating an apple, sharpening a pencil, pouring a cup of tea, cracking nuts, opening an envelope, pouring milk from a carton. Give each Scout a pencil and paper, and ask him to list the sound effects in the right order.

**Adventure trail**

Lay out a string trail between chairs (indoors) or bushes (outdoors) and hang a number of articles from the string. Choose items that can be identified by touch (tent peg, mug, torch), sound (bell, alarm clock) and smell (onion, orange, apple). Blindfold all the Scouts in the Patrol and when they have followed the trail, ask them to list the items in order.

**Shopping**

Give each Scout a list of goods on sale in your local shopping area – specifying brand names and size of packs. The Scouts are to find out, by looking in shop windows, which shops stock the items and the prices. When making out the list, make sure that all the items are displayed currently in the windows. Ask some of the shopkeepers to place a small item associated with the Scouts in their windows – a Scout Membership Badge, a buttonhole badge, a Group scarf, a Leader's tie. Tell the Scouts to look out for anything unusual in the windows – you may be surprised how few will spot the items you have placed in the windows specially for this activity.

# Shoot!

**Lemon shooter**

You will need: six elastic bands; two long garden canes; a plastic lemon; the tube part of an old biro-type pen; some kitchen roll paper; a short split cane; whipping twine; sticky tape.

Lash the two long canes together at one end as shown, using a series of tight overhand knots (half reefs) finished off with a reef knot. Make a tight ball of kitchen roll paper. Wedge this with the split cane between the two long canes close to the lashing and bind it tightly with several turns of sticky tape.

Join the elastic bands by slipping one through the other and then back through itself – you will need two strings of three bands each. Bind one end of each string to opposite sides of the tube part of the plastic pen with tape and lash the other ends of the strings to the tops of the canes. Unscrew the top from the plastic lemon and make a small hole at the opposite end.

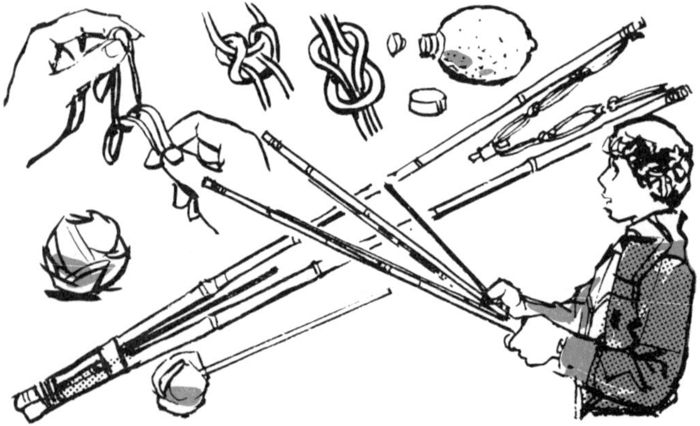

Pull the plastic tube down onto the split cane as far as it will go and slip the lemon onto the split cane. With the butt-end of the lemon shooter resting on your stomach, pull the lemon down, take aim and fire!

**Bouncing Bazooka**

You will need: three empty tins (with the tops and bottoms removed with a rotary can-opener to avoid jagged edges); five 4ft garden canes; a plastic lemon; the plastic top of a small aerosol container; two strings of four elastic bands; whipping twine; sticky tape.

Bind the cans to four canes with sticky tape as shown in the illustration. Fix the aerosol top to the strings of elastic bands with tape and lash the other ends of the strings to the tops of two of the canes on opposite sides so that the aerosol top hangs down inside the bazooka. Wedge the lemon on top of the spare cane – and fire away!

# Cycling

**Cycle obstacle course**
Here are some suggestions for a course, with obstacles and challenges to be completed along the way. Try this at your local camp site, in a nearby park or on a piece of rough ground. Devise your own obstacles using whatever materials you can find.

Scouts can use their own cycles or everyone could use the same old bike if the course is a rough one (and tough on brand new cycles!). Time each Scout over the course. Challenge Scouts from other Patrols to beat your best time.

**String rodeo**
Cut two lengths of sisal or string about 9m (30ft) long and tie the four ends to four large tin cans filled with stones or sand to weight them down. In the following events, riders lose one point when a wheel of the cycle touches the string.

•Straight ride. Lay the strings out parallel to each other 15cm (6ins) apart. Ride from one end to the other between the strings.

•Slow race. Spread the strings 1m (3ft) apart. Pedal down the course slowly without touching the ground or the string. Slowest time wins.

•Coasting. Start cycling 3m (9ft) back from where the string lines begin. Pedal rapidly up to the strings, but take your feet off the pedals as you reach the string and coast between the lines, without touching the ground or string. Longest coast wins.

•Quick stop. Ride up to one string from the side and brake to stop exactly 8cm (3ins) from the string.

# Make it!

**Wooden plaques**

You will need: some logs of 10–15cm (4–6ins) diameter; a saw; sandpaper; clear varnish; pencils; pressure or gas stove. You can make a burning iron by driving a 10cm (4ins) oval-headed nail into a block of wood (which becomes the handle).

Cut the log into pieces about 3cm (1in) thick – if you cut on the slant, you get more interesting shapes. Rub down one side with sandpaper to reveal the grain. Pencil words or initials on this side and then heat up the nail of your burning iron over the stove (taking care not to touch the nail when it gets hot). Now burn in the shapes of the letters in the wood. Varnish afterwards. Make plaques with the Patrol's name and places of camps.

**Turk's head woggles**

Use picture hanging cord in various colours – about 75cm (30ins) makes a double-stranded woggle on a 2.5cm (1in) bore.

*Scouts could make their own plaques with their names and the name of their Patrol burned into the wood.*

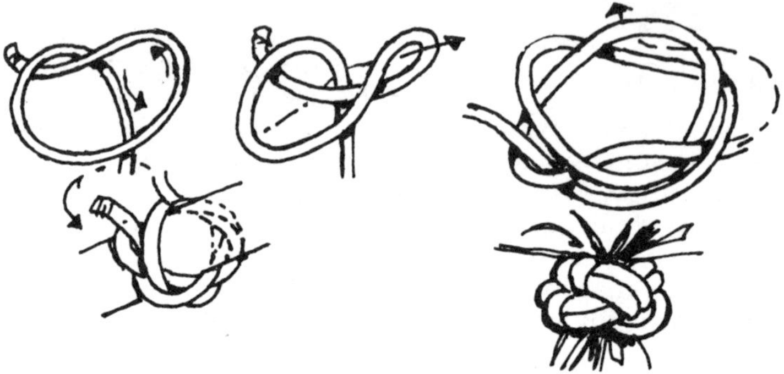

*Slip the cord over a cycle pump or broom handle for size as you make it. Keep the cord parallel to the strand being followed. Cut ends and sew off with heavy thread.*

## Indoor obstacle course

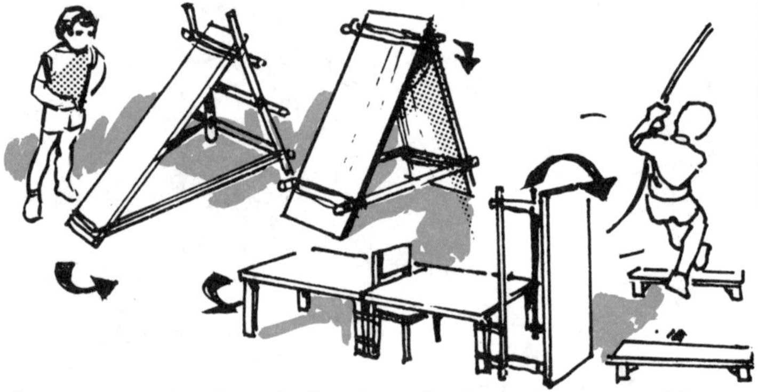

*Set up a course using planks of wood, pioneering spars, old trestle tables, ropes – anything you can find. Make sure the lashings are sound and then time each member of the Patrol around the course.*

# Outdoors

**Plaster casts**

You will need: plaster of Paris (dental plaster is best); a bowl; a spoon; water; a strip of fairly stiff card 5cm (2ins) wide by 30cm (12ins) long; a metal paper clip; string.

Look for an animal track in soft ground (the edge of a pond is a good place to start). Loop the strip of card into a collar, hold it in place with the paper clip and press it gently into the ground around the track.

Put a small quantity of water into the bowl and sprinkle in the plaster of Paris, stirring and adding more plaster until the mixture is like thick cream. Pour into the track until the plaster is about an inch deep inside the collar.

The plaster will take a few minutes to set (if you used ordinary plaster of Paris, you can speed up the setting process by adding a pinch of salt to the mixture). When the plaster shows signs of stiffening, press a small loop of string gently (and without disturbing the cast) into the back so that you can hang your completed cast on the wall.

**Estimation**

Give the Patrol a list of objects and ask them to estimate the height of each.

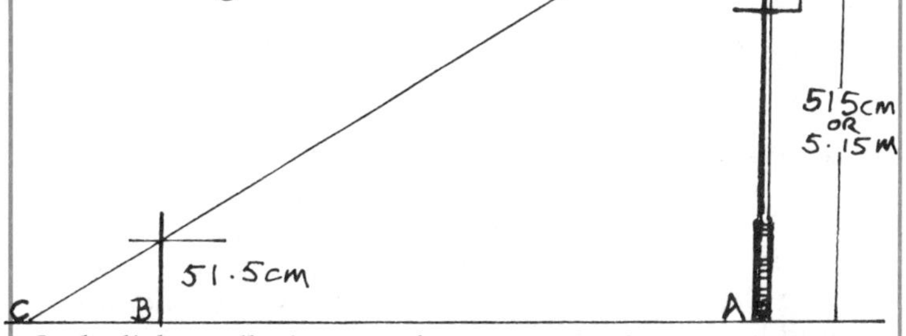


*In daylight: walk nine paces from A to B, and one more equal pace to C. Another Scout holds a stick upright at B. With your head down on the ground at C, look up past the stick to the top of the lamp post, while the other Scout moves his finger along the stick until it is in line with the top of the lamp-post. Measure the distance from the other Scout's finger to the ground in centimetres. Multiply by ten to give the height of the lamp post in centimetres. Divide by 100 to get the height in metres.*

*At night: tie two torches with spotlight beams to the end of a pole. Angle each torch so that the beams strike the top of the lamp post. Secure the torches in position, turn the pole so that the beams shine along the ground – and measure from the point on the ground where the beams meet back to the pole for the height of the post.*

# Just for fun . . .

**Knotting**

- The Patrol stands in a circle, each Scout with a knotting rope. The Patrol Leader calls out: "Tie a clove hitch around the left ankle of the Scout on your right". Try it again, but this time each Scout attempts to stop anyone putting a clove hitch around his left ankle.
- Scouts are in pairs, each with one hand behind his back. The pairs have to tie a number of knots, using their free hands only.
- Show the Scouts a length of rope with six knots tied in it. After a minute, take the rope away and ask the Scouts to tie the same knots in the correct order in their length of rope.

**Miniature pancakes**

Make a pancake mixture by breaking an egg into a mug and slowly adding 55g (2ozs) of plain flour and 15ml ($\frac{1}{4}$ pint) of milk, stirring until it is like thin cream. Beat in a small pat of butter and leave to stand for about an hour before you use it.

Give each Scout an almond, a match, a piece of wire about 25cm (10ins) long and another about 50cm (20ins) long and an aluminium foil cake dish. Ask each Scout to cook a pancake using the items you have given him, but the candle may not be used as a source of heat. Here's how to do it . . .

**Crash course**

*Make an Indian travois and race around a 50m (150ft) course on grass.*

*Build a pyramid – four, five or six Scouts high – and hold it for 30 seconds.*

*Follow a string trail – blindfolded with each Scout carrying a mug filled with water.*

*Build a tower – from plastic drinking cups or empty match boxes.*

Chapter 2

# The Patrol and the Troop

The idea of forming Scouts into Patrols, each with its own leader, might be seen merely as a convenient way to divide a large Troop into small units for games and activities. The Patrol System is much more than this: it is a method of helping a Scout to develop physically, mentally and spiritually through membership of a small group of friends. The members of the group learn to organise their own affairs and to accept increasing degrees of responsibility.

The Patrol System is not one of a number of different methods of running a Scout Troop – it is the only method. Sometimes the members of a Patrol will be of different ages with many interests, while in another Patrol the Scouts may be of similar age. The important point is that they are with friends in a Patrol of their liking. They will then naturally want to do things together as a Patrol away from Troop Night and in this way the Patrol will have a life of its own.

Patrols of mixed or similar ages consisting of groups of friends who get on well together are not necessarily going to produce balanced teams to be pitted against each other in games, but that is not the priority. What is important is that the Patrol is a happy one, where the Scouts have a sense of belonging, sharing the work that has to be done and supporting each other.

For these reasons it is worth taking a little time in deciding which Patrol a Cub Scout might join when he moves from the Pack. It is often best to keep friends together, for they will help each other to settle down. Scouts will sometimes bring their friends to join from outside the Movement and putting a friend into a different Patrol might not be the best thing to do. After all, they are friends outside the Troop, so why not build on that friendship within the Patrol?

There is often a temptation to allocate Scouts to Patrols and then to move them around from time to time simply to even up the numbers, but avoid this if you can. It may look neater on a wall chart and help with distributing food at summer camp, but eight friends working together in one Patrol and four in another is better than six Scouts in each with little in common.

Regular discussion at the Patrol Leaders' Council will be helpful in deciding which Patrols new Scouts might be invited to join. Friendships and interests will change as the months go by and the Patrol Leaders' Council should be ready to spot these and to suggest moves from Patrol to Patrol.

## The Patrol

- A Scout Patrol is made up of six or so Scouts – there may be more or there may be less.
- They will be friends who enjoy working and playing together.
- Members of a Patrol may live near each other (in a block of flats, a group of streets or a village), belong to the same club, or attend the same school or place of worship.
- The Scouts in the Patrol may be of different ages (with the older Scouts training and helping the younger

ones) or they might be of the same age (because they share an interest or happen to be a group of friends outside the Troop).

- Members of the Patrol share the responsibilities and the work that has to be done.
- Each Scout is involved in making decisions that affect himself and others: meeting as a Patrol-in-Council, they will put their ideas forward to the Patrol Leaders' Council.
- The Patrol is led by a Patrol Leader, who is appointed by the Scout Leader in consultation with the Patrol Leaders' Council and the members of the Patrol.
- An Assistant Patrol Leader is appointed by the Patrol Leader, with the approval of the Scout Leader and the Patrol Leaders' Council, to be the Patrol Leader's assistant and deputy.
- Patrol Leaders are generally drawn from amongst the older – and more experienced – Scouts in the Troop, but this does not have to be so. If a Patrol consists of younger Scouts, their Patrol Leader might be young. Similarly, if all the Scouts in a Patrol are keen on cycling, they may prefer to have a Patrol Leader with a bicycle – whatever his age.
- A Senior Patrol Leader may be appointed by the Scout Leader, after consultation with the Patrol Leaders' Council. A Senior Patrol Leader, whilst not having the responsibility of a Patrol, could chair the Patrol Leaders' Council. He could be the Scout Leader's right hand man, helping the Patrol Leaders in working with their Patrols – ensuring that all Scouts make progress through the Scout Section Training Programme, for example.

## Why belong?

Here are just a few reasons why Scouts enjoy belonging to Patrols, rather than merely teams in a large Troop.

- Young people have groups of friends of their own age or near to their own age. In the Scouts we should use this as an opportunity to offer training within a small group, where increasing degrees of responsibility can be given and leadership accepted.
- Within a Patrol a Scout will feel that he is needed. He will become involved in the activities of a small unit. His absence will be noted. He will learn to be concerned about those around him and find that others are prepared to support him, too. And all this would not be possible in a larger unit, such as the Troop.
- A Scout will know that he is being trusted, for every member of the Patrol will have a particular responsibility, and others will trust him and expect him to play his part. Later there will be opportunities to lead and to experience the full trust of others.
- Working within the Patrol, a Scout will learn different skills and enjoy new experiences with others – some from similar backgrounds and with others who are not. He will come to adjust to those who are quicker – and respect those who may be slower – than he is. He will grow in accepting success and disappointment, and in appreciating the skills of others. He will find that his own abilities are recognised and that there are those who will help him to do things he is not very good at a little better.
- A Patrol will have its own identity.

This will not only include a Patrol name, but also, say, a flag, a camp hat, a camp yell and so on. Ideally it will have a place of its own – a den where the members can meet together, but in reality this is often little more than a corner of the Scout Headquarters where they put their coats and sit on their Patrol box. No matter – it 'belongs' to the Patrol.

• A Patrol will have an indefinable spirit of its own, something that germinates amongst friends who enjoy each other's company. There must be flexibility about which Patrol a Scout is to join – and with how long he remains there. As we have said before, keep friends together but recognise that friendships change. Give a new Patrol time, but don't be so rigid that it never gets the chance to get off the ground.

## The Scouters' job

The Patrol System is not the easiest way to run a Troop – far from it! Teams of Scouts, of equal numbers and balanced ability, carrying out orders handed down from the Scout Leader, might produce a disciplined appearance to the casual visitor, but it is not the Scout Method. It might win every cup and trophy that is on offer, but it will hardly foster personal development, trust and an acceptance of responsibility.

For the Patrol System to have a chance of success, commitment to the ideal is needed – first, in the Scout Leader, and second, amongst every adult who comes into contact with the Patrols . . . from the Cub Scout Leader to the Group Scout Leader, and amongst the Scout Leader's team of Assistants, Instructors, Venture Scouts and so on. All should understand what the Patrol System is trying to achieve and give their backing to what is being done.

The Scouters' job is to . . .

• **Offer support and encouragement** to the Patrol Leader, who may need to be ahead with his own training and will want to be seen as one of the group of 'leaders' within the Troop – as Patrol Leaders and Scouters working together through the Patrol Leaders' Council.

• **Facilitate the making of decisions** and when they are made, to stand by them – and this is not always easy. A decision to buy some new games equipment may be a simple one to support, but when the majority of the Patrol Leaders' Council wants to replace the traditional Easter camp with a youth hostelling expedition, Scouters may find themselves objecting – for the wrong reasons.

• **Ensure that the Troop programme provides opportunities** for the Patrol System to work. Activities on Troop Night should be carried out in Patrols. At camp don't move Scouts from one Patrol to another just because there is space in a tent or room around a table. It may suit your administration to do so, but they have spent 50 weeks of the year learning to work and live together and that's far more important than the number of eggs you dish out for breakfast!

• **Enhance the place of the Patrol Leaders' Council** in the life of the Troop by making it clear that decisions are made there whilst, at the same time, ensuring that every Scout's point of view has the chance to be heard through the Patrol-in-Council.

• **Recognise that the Patrol System takes time** to work. If it has not been operating recently, three or four years may have to pass before a new generation of Scouts enjoys its benefits and produces its own Patrol Leaders. Be ready for disappointments, for every Troop has its ups and downs. Don't be tempted to fall back on running everything yourself for, with patience, you can ride it out and encourage a new start.

Lord Baden-Powell, the Founder of the Scouts, said: "Expect a great deal of your Patrol Leaders and nine times out of ten they will play up to your expectations, but if you are going always to nurse them and not to trust them to do things well, you will never get them to do anything on their own initiative."

## The Patrol Leaders' Council

The Patrol Leaders' Council is a meeting of those who share in running and leading the Scout Troop.

### Who goes?

The Patrol Leaders and, more often than not, the Scout Leader will go to Patrol Leaders' Council meetings. Occasionally, it's no bad thing for the Scout Leader not to be present for all or part of the session, for there will be times when the Patrol Leaders want to talk on their own (and the Scouters have this same opportunity at Group Scouters' Meetings).

From time to time Assistant Patrol Leaders are invited to the meetings – in some Troops they take it in turn to come along and in other (and smaller) Troops they attend more regularly. It gives them a chance to see how the Council works, to make a contribution and to prepare for the time when they may become Patrol Leaders.

Whether or not Assistant Scout Leaders take part is a matter for your Troop to decide. Often they will have something to add to the discussion and their views will be helpful, so perhaps it is best for them to take turns (if there is more than one Assistant) or to come when a topic in which they have a particular interest is under debate. The same applies to Venture Scouts and Instructors who are working with the Troop.

Other Scouts in the Troop may come to the Patrol Leaders' Council by invitation. For example, if the Council is discussing canoeing activities in the Troop, one or two Scouts who are keen on canoeing might join in – the Patrol Leaders will benefit from their expertise and the Scouts who know about these things will feel that their views are being taken into account. Similarly, Scouts working for the Leadership Award need to attend at least one meeting of the Patrol Leaders' Council and take responsibility for carrying out some of the decisions that are made – and this includes all older Scouts, not just Patrol Leaders and Assistants.

In the same way, other Scouters might be invited to all or part of a meeting. The Cub Scout Leader could brief the Patrol Leaders on the Cub Scouts who are taking their Link Badge before they meet the boys and invite them to join a Patrol. Similarly, the Venture Scout Leader and members of the Unit Executive Committee could attend a Council meeting – to plan joint activities with the Unit or to talk about those Scouts who will shortly go into the Unit.

As a rule of thumb, the Patrol Leaders would vote if there are differing views on something, but the Scout Leader would not do so. Assistant Scout Leaders and visitors would not vote. The Scout Leader is there to guide and advise, particularly in matters of safety.

There are no hard and fast rules. Each Patrol Leaders' Council should run its affairs in the way that works best for them and to the benefit of the Patrols in the Troop.

## What it does

The Patrol Leaders' Council . . .

- **Meets regularly,** perhaps once a month, and at other times when necessary.
- **Plans** programmes of activities, training, camps and expeditions for the Patrols and the Troop.
- **Encourages** Scouts to take advantage of the Scout Section Training Programme and provides opportunities for them to do so.
- **Takes an interest** in the transfer of Cub Scouts from the Pack and the recruitment of new Scouts from outside, and helps them to settle into the Troop.
- **Works** with the Venture Scout Unit Executive Committee in planning training and activities for older Scouts and for specialist groups or Patrols within the Troop. Sometimes Venture Scouts will act as instructors: at others the activities may be joint with Scouts and Venture Scouts taking part.
- **Ensures** that the Patrol System is working effectively in the Troop.
- **Assesses** the individual Scout's overall achievement for the Scout, Pathfinder, Explorer and Chief Scout's Awards and agrees that the Award should be presented. Likewise for the Patrol Activity Award and the Leadership Award.
- **Sets standards** to be achieved in the Scout Section Training Programme and discusses these with individual Scouts.
- **Is responsible** for the administration of Patrol and Troop funds.
- **Discusses** the appointment of Patrol Leaders and Assistant Patrol Leaders.

## The Council in action!

The following are suggestions for ways in which the Patrol Leaders' Council might run its affairs. Before we do so, however, your Troop may not have a Patrol Leaders' Council working at the moment – and you will want to know how to get started. The ideas that follow will take some time to achieve and it's best to get going in a small way.

Begin by calling a meeting of the Patrol Leaders to discuss one item – your next camp or an activity the Troop is running. At this first meeting the Scout Leader might act as chairman, with a Patrol Leader making a note of the decisions that are made. Hold another meeting after the camp or event – to discuss how it went and to plan something else. At this meeting one of the Patrol Leaders should act as chairman, with the Scout Leader offering advice on how the chairman handled things when the meeting is over.

Once you have had some successful meetings – and camps and events – both the Scout Leader and Patrol Leaders will gain in confidence and you can start adding items to the agenda.

Don't be put off by the following suggestions. They will work in time, but start small, build confidence and aim for something on these lines . . . eventually.

- The Patrol Leaders' Council needs a chairman, who might be the Senior Patrol Leader (if you have one) or a Patrol Leader elected by the others (perhaps for a set time limit of a few months so that others take a turn).
- A Patrol Leader acts as Secretary, preparing the agenda of items to be discussed (and, if possible, giving members a copy beforehand), records the decisions made and sees that action is taken.
- Another Patrol Leader is the Treasurer, keeping a note of funds held by the Patrols and recording details of the Troop's funds.
- Follow usual committee procedures without being too formal. Meetings should not last too long, but allow sufficient time for everyone to contribute (and never give the impression that you want to get the meeting over as quickly as possible).
- Where the Council meets is something for discussion. A room in the Headquarters may be available or the Council might prefer to hold meetings in one of their homes.
- Patrol Leaders represent their Patrols. The Patrol Leaders' own views are important – and should be heard – but, in addition, they have a responsibility to carry forward into the discussion the opinions of the Scouts in their Patrols.

## Agenda for a Patrol Leaders' Council

Opening prayer.
Apologies for absence.
Minutes of the last meeting.
Matters arising not covered by the agenda.
Items for discussion – programme planning, Scouts' progress in Awards and badges, transfers from Pack and into Unit, finance, training programme, Troop and Patrol organisation.
Any other business.
Date and place of next meeting.
Closing prayer.

The Scout Leader may sometimes feel that he is walking a tightrope at the Patrol Leaders' Council – and that is to be expected. He will try to help the Patrol Leaders to find ways of carrying out their plans and to solve problems as they arise, while encouraging them to take opportunities that may not always be clear to them. He helps to turn plans into reality by drawing on past experience and through finding adult support and equipment.

At times the Patrol Leaders may be too ambitious – and at others not ambitious enough! Safety may be of greater concern to the Scout Leader and the parents. The Scout Leader may need to offer advice on safety and should not be afraid to sound a note of caution when it is needed. If the right spirit of working together exists in the Patrol Leaders' Council that will be expected – and accepted.

If an activity sounds too costly for some of the parents, the Scout Leader should explain why this might be so and suggest alternatives. He may have to point out that, by reason of age or due to other factors, something they are planning is not legal or against the rules of the Association.

The Scout Method encourages young people to make their own decisions, guided by adult leaders. At the Patrol Leaders' Council guidance – and not dictatorship – is the essence, but it may prove to be a balancing act requiring diplomacy, tact and understanding.

## Action 2

Cooking a snack or a full meal gets the members of the Patrol together. Meet at a nearby camp site, in someone's garden or on a piece of waste ground where you have permission to cook.

# Charcoal cooking

An old metal dustbin lid or metal tray raised off the ground on some bricks is the fireplace. Put a layer of sand or a double thickness of cooking foil down first so that the heat does not scorch the grass.

You can buy charcoal and firelighters in camping and outdoor shops. Light the fire at least an hour before you want to cook. Put a firelighter in the centre of the lid or tray and surround this with small pieces of charcoal. Light the firelighter and let it catch the charcoal, gradually adding more (and larger) pieces of charcoal.

After about five minutes use an air-bed pump to fan the flames gently – this will help to spread the fire through the charcoal.

**What to cook?**

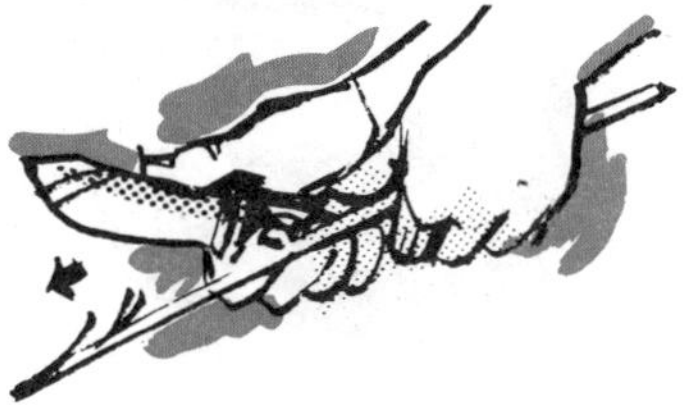

*Peel a green stick (not laurel or yew), cutting away from the hand holding the stick.*

*Spear some small pieces of meat, onion, carrot, mushroom, swede, potato, tomato and any other vegetables you have available onto a green stick. Hold the kebab above the charcoal, slowly turning the stick as it cooks.*

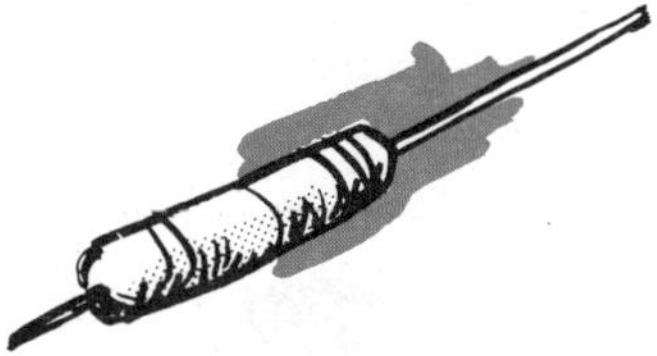

*Spear through a sausage lengthways and hold it over the hot charcoal to cook.*

*Mix flour and water (with a pinch of salt) into a thick paste. Roll between your hands into a 'snake' shape and wrap it around a green stick. Cook over the charcoal, turning as you do so to avoid burning. When cooked, your 'twist' should slide cleanly off the green stick. Spread with butter and jam before eating.*

# Foil cooking

Experiment with cooking food wrapped inside aluminium cooking foil – ideal with a charcoal fire or a wood fire that has burned down to the embers (flames will granulate the foil, making holes and allowing the food to burn).

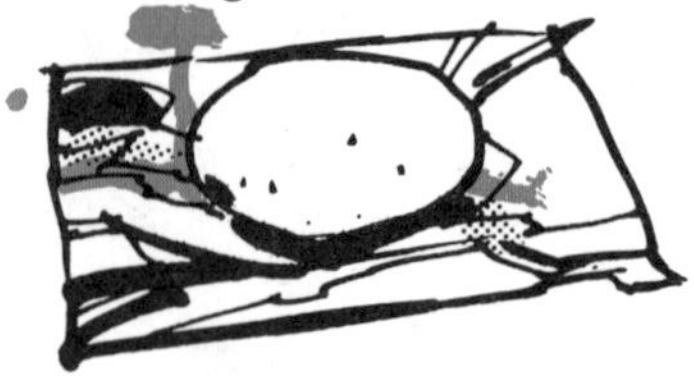

*Place a potato – still in its skin – in the centre of a piece of aluminium cooking foil.*

*Bring two sides of the foil together and make two folds of 2½cm (1in), leaving a small air space above the potato.*

*Fold over the ends of the foil in the same way, leaving a small amount of air trapped inside. Now place the foil-wrapped potato in the embers to cook slowly.*

*Wrap other foods in foil in the same way – sausages (with a little onion), an apple (with the core removed and the centre filled with currants, a little sugar and a pat of butter) or a banana.*

*Now try a complete meal in foil. Slice some onion rings and put these down first as a 'bed' for the rest of the food (if anything is going to burn, let it be the onions!). Put meat or sausages on top. Cut up the vegetables into thin slices – carrots take three times as long to cook as potatoes, so the carrot slices should be one third the thickness of the slices of potato. Bring the sides and ends of the foil together – and remember to leave a small air space over the food.*

## Experiment

- Is there a difference between tea made in a warmed teapot and a cold one?
- Does it make any difference to the taste if you have milk in the cup before you pour the tea – or if you add the milk after pouring?
- How long does it take to make a cup of tea on a pressure stove or a camp gas stove – taking the time from the moment you start to light the stove? Work out the cost of fuel used during this time by each stove. Which is the cheapest and which the quickest method?

# Scavenge hunt

These are easy to arrange and fun to take part in. Prepare a list of things for pairs of Scouts to find and set a time when the game is over and everyone is to be back at your base.

Take care in preparing the list that you are not asking Scouts to bring back anything that will cause damage or distress to members of the public. A bus ticket might be easy to find and will not cause anyone distress; asking your Scouts to bring back a tulip could result in someone's garden being invaded – and an irate householder.

In the same way, asking Scouts to collect the signatures of a number of Scouters or Commissioners is fine (although it's best to warn those who may be approached in advance), but the ticket collector at your local railway station may not take too kindly to the same request from Scout after Scout – especially if a rush hour train has arrived when they turn up!

Here are some suggestions for things you might list in a scavenge hunt – and they will spark off ideas of your own, which will be far better:

- An egg yolk without the white;
- A hot cup of tea;
- Some ice;
- A lighted candle;
- A complete set of British coins;
- A piece of brass;
- A newspaper published yesterday;
- A picture of the Queen;
- A piece of homework for which a Scout got full marks;
- Something from France;
- Leaves from six trees which can be identified;
- A message written in Morse.

# Know your town

**Directions**

Give your Patrol practice in directing people to important places in your home area. Write out a list of starting points and destinations, and ask each Scout to work out the quickest route on foot, by public transport and in a car. Send each Scout out to try one of the routes and to report back on his findings.

**Survey**

Carry out a survey of facilities for the elderly or handicapped in your home area. For example, how many shops and public buildings have ramps to allow wheelchair users to enter?

**Timetables**

Collect local bus and train timetables. Ask your Scouts to go through these to find out details of early morning, late-night and all-night services. Work out the best way to get from place to place at these times. Check the cost of tickets at the bus and railway stations. Which is the cheapest method of transport?

**Photographs**

Take your own photographs or collect sketches and pictures in the local newspapers of landmarks – an unusual gate, a corner of the frontage of a large store, a monument, a church doorway. Ask your Scouts to go out in pairs and find each landmark – and then to discover a little more about the building. Meet up after an agreed time to discuss what they found out.

# Mapping

**Quiz**

Give each pair of Scouts an Ordnance Survey map of your home area, pencils and paper. Read out a set of questions like these:

- From the top of the hill at grid reference . . . and looking south-west, what prominent landmark would you see?
- Name the conventional sign at grid reference . . .
- Find the grid references of three churches with spires.
- If distance was no object, which route would you take between A and B so that most of your journey on a bicycle was downhill?

**Tape recorder hike**

This is something that one or two older Scouts in the Patrol might prepare for the younger members. Take a portable tape recorder and walk for three or four miles from an agreed point. As you walk, talk into the tape recorder, describing the things you see and the directions in which you turn. Give each Scout a map of the area and tell them where the hike started – and as the tape is played, let them work out the route that was followed.

**Bearings**

Give each pair of Scouts a compass and a list of landmarks. Ask them to take a compass bearing on each landmark from a point stated in the list.

- Indoors – list a series of objects around the room.
- In town – landmarks from the tops of high buildings that are open to the public; traffic lights, telegraph poles, shops etc., at a cross-roads; trees and buildings in parks.
- In the country – landmarks from the tops of hills, across open fields, on the edge of a village or marked trees around a field or clearing in a wood.

# Just for fun

From time to time challenge the Scouts in your Patrol to try something new, to practise a skill or to prepare something in the days before your next Patrol meeting – and start the meeting with each Scout demonstrating what he has done.

- With just one hand . . . peel an orange; button up your shirt and put on a tie; set an alarm clock; sew on a button; tie a shoelace.
- Collect one naturally-occuring item for each letter of the alphabet.
- Cook an egg in an orange skin and persuade a friend to eat it.
- Write a Patrol song and accompany yourself as you sing it on a home-made musical instrument.
- Devise a game for the Patrol to play.
- Make a working model of a camp shower.
- Make fire by friction.
- Make your own chopsticks and use them to eat some boiled rice.
- Recite the alphabet backwards from memory.
- Construct an egg timer.
- Make a scarecrow with moving parts that can be operated from a distance of 3m (10ft).
- Prepare a short act of worship to end your Patrol meeting.
- Pitch a tent upside down.

Chapter 3

# The Troop

For the Scout Method to be successful, we should look on the Scout Troop as a collection of Patrols, rather than as an entity in itself. Of course, the Troop exists with a life of its own (and people locally will talk about the Troop and want to see it thrive), but for those closely involved the Troop is a number of Patrols, sometimes meeting as Patrols, but coming together as a Troop for a wider range of activities than might be possible if they met apart all the time.

The Troop offers many opportunities for Scouts to:

•**Meet others.** In addition to joining the members of other Patrols in the Troop for activities, they will meet Scouts from other Troops at District and County courses and events. They will be with Scouts who have similar interests to their own (and, however hard we try, that is not always possible within the Patrol. Minority interests may be met in the Troop, but stand a better chance in

the District and County. How many really keen meteorologists or horse riders are in your Patrol or Troop?).

For those of your Patrols which are of mixed age ranges, Troop Night is the chance for Scouts of the same age to be together for a change, while some District and County activities and training courses will be arranged for Scouts of a particular age and development. A County camp will draw Scouts from a wider cross-section of the community than will be found in a single Patrol and here a Scout will learn to work with others from different backgrounds and environments. There are opportunities, too, for joint activities with other organisations – The Boys' Brigade, the Girl Guides, the youth club down the road and so on – and with Scouts from other countries. In experiences such as these, Scouts learn to understand and respect the points of view of others far beyond their own circle of family and friends.

•**Develop a competitive spirit.** Within the Patrol a Scout will share the tasks, support others and – in turn – be offered support, but we should recognise that we live in a competitive world. Meeting the challenge of competition (and, sometimes, coming to terms with it) may not arise within a small Patrol but it happens when a number of Patrols meet together. This is not to say that all Troop activities will be competitive: Scouts from different Patrols may decide to work on a Collective Achievement Badge and here they would not be competing against each other – quite the reverse, in fact.

It is in the games and competitions where Scouts will identify with their Patrol, work as part of that team and accept personal responsibility within that team for success or otherwise.

•**Put the Patrol System into action.** This will be achieved through the Patrol Leaders' Council. The Patrol Leaders and Scouters accept responsibility for programmes, training and leadership.

•**Enjoy a wider range of activities.** Numbers, cost and equipment will mean that the Patrol's programme may not be enough on its own – particularly for those who want to try more adventurous pursuits and for those older Scouts who find being with younger Scouts tends to pall after a time. Troop activities should be planned with this in mind – not substituting for those things that Patrols can enjoy as a unit, but rather extending the programme and expanding its scope. The District and County should be looking for opportunities to go even wider and, again, not duplicate or take over those things that are better done in the Patrol or the Troop.

•**Work with adults.** The Scout Method is a combination of young people working on their own and with adults. Learning by doing is the key phrase and Patrols, small groups and individuals should be encouraged to do things on their own. The Scouter's job is to make sure that they have adequate equipment, training and (where necessary) instructors. The Scout Leader needs to be satisfied on safety and that parents are aware of what is happening and are in agreement. It is a fact that we learn by our mistakes, but if we are not motivated to try out new experiences we may never have the opportunity to do just that. Yet another tightrope for the Scouter to walk is one between providing guidance and support (which is the Scout Method) and taking over completely (which is not).

Scouters will work through the Patrol Leaders in helping them to run programmes, offer training and in supporting their Scouts. That is the Scouters' prime function, but it is not the only one. Learning to work with people around your own age is one thing, but in preparing Scouts for life in their community (and beyond) we need to involve them with adults.

For the Cub Scout (who is used to his parents and Cub Scouters being on hand to pick him up if he trips) the presence of adults on Troop Night and looking in for a few minutes at a Patrol meeting will be reassuring. At the other end of the scale, an older Scout working with the Group Quartermaster on equipment repairs, with the Unit in running a joint activity or with members of the Group Council on fund raising will find the company of adults satisfying for quite different reasons – he will be accepted as part of an adult group and respond to a

more adult approach than he might have found elsewhere.

Scouters cannot hope to know every boy really well, but they should aim to be on friendly terms with them all. Some will require more direct help from adults than others. A few will relate more easily to adults than to Scouts of their own age or a Patrol Leader who may be younger or just a little older. Those with particular personal problems may demand a disproportionate amount of the Scouters' time. Getting the balance right, like so many things, comes with experience.

•**Involve the handicapped.** Scouts who are handicapped will want to join in with everything that is going on. Much will depend on the handicap and, whilst some may be able to take a full part, others might not. Some will need help to cope with their disability, but with the Patrol Leader's support everyone in the Patrol will gain from having a member with a handicap. Whenever possible, Scouts with a handicap should work alongside the rest of the Patrol, but sometimes extra adult support may be necessary to allow this to happen. Parents and others in day to day contact with the handicapped will be able to tell you just how much help they need and how they can contribute to Patrol and Troop life. In addition, specialist Commissioners in the District and County are there to give advice when needed.

## The Scout Leader

It is the easiest thing in the world for an adult to offer to help a Patrol with some badgework – and to end up taking out a warrant, running the Troop, collecting the jumble and being out every night of the week! Being a Scout Leader will involve more than one night a week at Troop Meeting (and don't listen to anyone who tells you otherwise!), but it does not have to be a seven-day-a-week drudge.

Scout Leaders need to think out their priorities to fit in with (and not to over-ride) their commitments at home, at work and in the community. A Scout Leader who is away from home too much may find his wife and children are growing away from him, no longer feeling that he is interested in what goes on behind the front door – unless it has 'Scouts' written all over it. A housewife running a Scout Troop may receive the backing of husband and family at the start, but if the cooking and housework are no longer shared, they could react against her . . . and against the Scouts. It is important to keep things in proportion.

It is just the same with other adults who help with the Troop and there is a danger, too, that we overlook the fact that the Troop cannot be the number one priority of Patrol Leaders and their Scouts. Family and school come first, and there will be other interests apart from Scouting – which is not the only organisation requiring a commitment. Scouts who have paper rounds, who belong to a church choir, are members of a football team or who play in the school orchestra will find that the times of Scout activities may clash. We cannot insist that Scout activities must come first nor should we always be appealing to loyalty to the Patrol or Troop – the football team has just as much right to that as the Scouts. Scouts have to make choices as they move into adult life and we can help them to do so.

Arranging a weekend camp near enough so that a Scout can get back to take his place in the church choir is a helpful compromise. Insisting that he stays at camp produces confrontation – and both the choir and the Scouts may be the losers. If a Scout is committed to play football every Saturday morning in the season, we can hardly expect him to turn up for a Patrol meeting at that time. When a Scout decides to join a judo club meeting on the same night as the Troop, choices have to be made, without rancour or hard feelings.

Every Scout Leader will have his own list of the things with which he becomes involved and it might look like this:

- You will meet most weeks with the Scouts in the Troop – either calling in at their Patrol meetings or at a Troop Night.
- You will be in regular touch with the Patrol Leaders, helping them to run their Patrols and to make sure that their Patrols have lives of their own.
- You will clearly be looking out for

potential Patrol Leaders (who will not necessarily be the oldest Scouts in the Troop), making sure that they are getting the right training and experience.

- You will meet with your Assistant Scout Leaders and other adults who help – planning, discussing and assessing progress.
- You will go to Patrol Leaders' Council meetings – for all or part of the time – where Patrol and Troop programmes are planned.
- You will become involved in day, weekend and longer activities. How many will be up to the Patrol Leaders' Council to decide (and here home, work/school and community commitments will play a part). A day activity once a month, a weekend activity every two or three months and a longer camp or expedition once a year is a good starting point.
- You will be involved with other parts of the Group – taking an interest in the Beaver Colony, visiting the Pack and Unit, attending Group Scouters' Meetings and meetings of the Group Executive Committee. There will be fund raising and other Group social events that you will want to go to – although these should be organised and run by members of the Group Council and not by the Scouters.
- You will meet with other Leaders in the District and County – exchanging ideas and joining with others to arrange (and sometimes help to run) activities for Scouts in all the Troops locally, such as badge courses, activity days and Patrol Leaders' training courses.
- You will be involved in training for the job you have undertaken.
- Your religious observance is a personal priority, but you will also be concerned to ensure that every Scout has the opportunity to develop his own faith.

## Not alone!

You cannot – and should not – attempt to do all this alone. As a Scout Leader you need a team of people to help you. . .

- **Patrol Leaders.** Wherever possible work through your Patrol Leaders. It may seem more efficient to stand before the Troop, giving out reams of paper and making announcements into the air, but you usurp your Patrol Leaders every time you do so. Pass information to your Scouts through their Patrol Leaders. Sometimes this may have to be in the form of a written note to be certain that parents have details of the whereabouts and cost of camps and the like, but give responsibility to the Patrol Leaders to inform their Patrols and they will be more inclined to encourage their Scouts to take part.

Use the Patrol Leaders' Council to the full – planning programmes, assessing standards, making awards for achievement – making it clear in all that you do that these things are decided by the Council and not by you alone. At times this will ease your burden, at others it will increase it – but it is the Scout Method.

- **Assistant Scout Leaders.** Assistants may be appointed from the age of eighteen onwards, to work with the Scout Leader and to act as his deputy. Assistants need to be given specific responsibilities (which may change from time to time) for parts of the Troop programme. One Assistant might work with the Patrol Leaders helping new members of the Troop to settle in. Another could be responsible for arranging activities for older Scouts. An Assistant who is keen on water activities could specialise in this aspect of the programme – taking training (if necessary) and not only extending the scope of the Troop's water activities, but also offering help to other Troops in the District.

If you are fortunate enough to have more than one Assistant Scout Leader each will want to feel that he or she has a worthwhile job to do. Don't expect them to come to Troop Night to watch you doing everything (for they will end up sitting on the radiators with a look of boredom that should tell you they won't be coming next week!). The other danger is that if Assistants do not have specific responsibilities, they will take over jobs that should be done by the Patrol Leaders. An Assistant who comes to Troop Night, helps with inspection, counts up the subscriptions and runs a team game might feel there are better ways to pass an evening. An Assistant who misses every other Troop Night and spends a half a day at the weekend training a

few Scouts in canoeing could feel that there is a purpose in being involved.

•**Venture Scouts.** It is much the same with Venture Scouts who want to work with the Troop. Find out what they are good at and enjoy doing – and use their talents – but don't let them become overgrown Patrol Leaders. A Troop that does not give its Patrol Leaders responsibility and allows Assistant Scout Leaders and Venture Scouts to do their jobs for them will find that the Patrol Leaders leave. Other Scouts in the Troop – and not only the older ones – may be ready to accept some responsibility, too, or they will become bored and find fulfilment elsewhere. Some Scouts never get the chance to become Patrol Leaders (often through no fault of their own, but simply because there are only so many Patrols). Scouting is hardly satisfying to a fourteen-year-old who is treated as if he is still ten. A Troop with a team of Assistants and Venture Scouts running everything should not be surprised if the average age of its Scouts starts to go down – for the older Scouts will show their feelings with their feet!

•**Other Leaders in the Group.** The Scouters of the Group are a team working with the Group Scout Leader – and not individuals running their Sections in isolation. The Scout Leader will work with the Cub Scout Leader (on the Link Badge with Cubs moving into the Troop), with the Venture Scout Leader (on joint activities for older Scouts and on transfers into the Unit) and with all Leaders (on Group camps, shows or similar events you may decide to run).

•**Administrators.** Look around for adults – perhaps with limited time to spare – who will take over some of the paperwork (records, reports, letters, collecting subscriptions and managing the accounts).
•**Instructors.** Again, these may be people with limited time but with expertise in particular activities. Some may wish to be more fully involved and wear uniform; others will help occasionally.
•**Parents.** Find out the hobbies, interests and skills of the parents of your Scouts. Direct requests for specific help are the most effective. Parents may be happier working with a Patrol or a small group of Scouts – helping them to learn to cook, with cycle or car maintenance or simply with transport.
•**Outside the Group.** The local youth officer may suggest instructors for some activities and offer equipment on loan. Other organisations specialising in particular activities may be willing to help with instruction and training courses (first aid, riding, sailing and so on).

If an adult from outside the Group offers help, the Group Scout Leader should be fully informed im-

mediately so that he may advise the District Commissioner, who will enquire about any previous involvement with Scouting.
•**The Scout District and County.** The District Scout Fellowship supports Scouting in a variety of ways and amongst the members you may find some who would welcome the chance to help with programmes in your Patrols and Troop from time to time. The District and County will offer:
•The help and advice of your Assistant District Commissioners and Assistant County Commissioners for Scouts, with whom the Scout Leader will be in regular touch.
•Similar help when needed from Commissioners and Advisers concerned with training, activities, handicapped Scouts, water and air activities and international contacts.
•Training courses – for Patrol Leaders and Scouters.
•Proficiency Badge courses.
•Facilities on camp sites and at activity centres.
•Specialist activities – especially for older Scouts.

The reference section at the end of this book includes brief notes about the services provided by the Association's Headquarters.

## Managing the Troop

It is easy to become submerged beneath paperwork, which should be sufficient to suppport the activities of the Troop but not replace them by the amount of time it takes to keep the records up to date. Keep the paperwork to the minimum needed for efficiency and involve others in this side of things.

•**Records.** Keep a card to record each Scout's personal details and progress. Every Scout should retain his own *Scout Record Book* in which he notes his progress through the training scheme. Troop progress wallcharts are useful (provided they are kept up to date), but Patrol charts are best (and can be marked up by a Scout in the Patrol).

•**Programme material.** You will collect a range of games and activity books (and there is a suggested list to get started with at the end of this book), published within and outside the Association. Keep a ring binder with SCOUTING supplements and handouts collected on training courses.

The training manual ring binder will contain notes you have made on courses and the handouts you were given. Keep an information folder with up to date copies of District and County newsletters, the *Information from Headquarters* pages in SCOUTING Magazine, programme ideas clipped from newspapers, magazines, comics and so on.

•**Money.** The Patrol Leaders' Council is responsible for Troop funds and may decide to fix a weekly or monthly subscription – part of which goes into Troop funds (for badges, equipment and the like) with the balance for Patrol funds (for use within the Patrol for their activities and equipment). In some Troops a percentage of the subscription goes straight into the Group account – towards the Membership Subscription or into a camp account. A simple accounting system is needed which should be agreed with the Group Treasurer, who will wish to see the accounts from time to time and include them in his annual audit.

•**Equipment inventory.** The Patrols and the Troop need equipment for their games and activities. It is best if each Patrol has a box in which to keep items for training and activities (compass, maps, knotting ropes, cooking canteen, hand-axe, pencils, felt pens, paper, training books and so on) whilst the Troop keeps the games equipment (tennis balls, footballs, blindfolds). Tentage, pioneering equipment, canoes and other specialist gear is best held by the Scout Group, so that all Sections can use it. Scouts should take part in some of the Group's fund raising activities for new and replacement equipment, and should also assist regularly in its maintenance as part of their training.

•**Newsletters.** If the Group has a newsletter or magazine, use it to let people know what the Patrols and the Troop are doing. If not, have an occasional newsletter to the parents giving them plenty of notice of dates of activities and camps, and keeping them informed about progress and achievements.

## Ceremonies

Ceremonies should be brief and to the point and should mean something to the people who are taking part. Everyone involved should know beforehand what they are expected to do and say.

It may be appropriate for parents to be invited to some ceremonies. When awards are being made, make sure that everyone understands what has gone into the achievement. The Group Scout Leader should be encouraged to attend and invited to play a part in some ceremonies. In the same way, other Leaders in the Group may like to be present from time to time.

The notes that follow are for guidance only. Troops and Groups will have their own traditions and that's fine – just as long as the ceremony is understood by those taking part.

## Going-up

The Group Scouters' Meeting is the place to decide the most convenient times for Going-up Ceremonies from the Pack to the Troop, and from the Troop to the Unit. The end of a Pack Meeting (when the Troop attend) might be best for a Cub Scout Going-up or the end of a Troop Meeting (with the Unit present) for a Going-up to the Venture Scouts. If the whole Group is together – for a religious service or camp – that could be an ideal time, emphasising that the Scout Group is like a family with all Sections taking an interest in the progress of members.

The Pack and Troop (or Troop and Unit) are each in horse-shoe formation, standing opposite one another, with open ends to the centre. The Group Scout Leader briefly explains what is going to happen. The Cub Scout stands in front of the Cub Scout Leader, who thanks him for what he has done in the Pack and wishes him well in the Troop. Both walk forward to the dividing line, where the Scout Leader and the Cub Scout's future Patrol Leader are waiting to greet him.

The Scout Leader welcomes the Cub Scout and his Patrol Leader takes him to meet his new Patrol.

The Group Scout Leader leads the Group in a suitable yell.

The ceremony for a Scout moving into the Unit is similar, involving the Scout Leader, the Venture Scout Leader and the Chairman of the Unit Executive Committee.

If all Sections of the Group are present, a large circle is probably the best formation.

## Investiture

If a Cub Scout has completed his Link Badge, he may be invested as a Scout immediately following the Going-up Ceremony. A Cub Scout who is being invested as a Scout wears his Group scarf during the Investiture. He has never ceased being a member of the Group and is, therefore, entitled to wear it. Only if a boy completely new to Scouting or a Cub Scout from another Group is being invested should the Group Scout Leader present him with his Group scarf during the ceremony.

The Patrols stand in a horse-shoe with the Scouters at the open end. The Patrol Leader brings forward the member of his Patrol who is to be invested and both stand in front of the Scout Leader. The Scout Leader then has a short – but personal – conversation with the new Scout, asking him if he knows what his honour is, if he knows, understands and accepts the Scout Law, and if he can be trusted on his honour to keep the Scout Promise.

The Scout Leader brings the Troop to the alert and if parents are present he should ask them to stand as well. All invested Scouts and the Scout who is being invested make the Scout Sign. In some Troops a Patrol Leader will move forward at this point and lower the Troop flag between the Scout Leader and the Scout who is to be invested, so that the staff is horizontal (taking care that the flag itself does not touch the ground). As the Promise is made both the new Scout and the Scout Leader place their left hands on the flag.

The Scout Leader asks the new Scout to make the Scout Promise to him, phrase by phrase: "On my honour, I promise . . . that I will do my best . . . to do my duty to God . . . and to the Queen . . . to help other people . . . and to keep the Scout Law".

At the end of the Promise, the Scout Leader and the Scout remove their hands from the flag and all return to the alert. Shaking hands with the new Scout, the Scout Leader says that he trusts him to keep that Promise and welcomes him as a Scout in the worldwide brotherhood of Scouts (but if the Scout has not previously been a Cub Scout, he would welcome him as a 'member of the worldwide brotherhood of Scouts').

The Scout Leader hands the Scout his badges and his Patrol Leader gives him his Patrol badge. The Group Scout Leader welcomes him as a Scout in the Group and then presents his scarf if he has not previously been a member of the Group. The ceremony ends with a yell and the Patrol Leader and Scout return to their Patrol.

If the Scout's parents are present make them feel comfortable before, during and after the ceremony – and this applies not only at an Investiture, but whenever parents are invited to be present when an award is made. Provide chairs for them to sit on, explain beforehand that you would like them to stand for the ceremony and offer tea or coffee afterwards so that you have the chance to talk informally. Explain, too, that if they have made the Scout Promise at some time, they are welcome to make the Scout Sign at the appropriate time during the ceremony.

## Presentation of badges and awards

These short ceremonies are usually held at the end of a Troop Meeting, but from time to time a Group Open Evening or Going-up Ceremony might be a suitable occasion for achievements to be marked in this way.

It is important to emphasise the involvement of Patrol Leaders in the training that is necessary for badges and awards, and the fact that such awards are made by the Patrol Leaders' Council. Presentation ceremonies are an opportunity to make that point.

The Patrols are in a horse-shoe. Scouts come forward from their Patrols to the Scout Leader who makes the presentation. The Scout's Patrol Leader might come forward with the Scout or you may decide that all members of the Patrol Leaders' Council should stand with the Scout Leader as the badges are presented. In a few words, the Scout Leader or a Patrol Leader should explain what the Scout has achieved.

More prominence should be given to the presentation of a Chief Scout's Award – which falls into two parts. The badge might be presented at a Troop Meeting, but preferably at a suitable event that is attended by other members of the Group (an Open Evening or after a religious service, for example). The badge should be presented by the District Commissioner or if he is unable to be present, by the Assistant

District Comissioner (Scouts). Arrangements are made within Counties for Chief Scout's Award Receptions, where the County Commissioner or his nominee will present the Chief Scout's Award Certificate.

## Patrol Leaders and Assistant Patrol Leaders

When the appointment of a Patrol Leader or Assistant Patrol Leader is agreed by the Patrol Leaders' Council, the appropriate badge is presented by the Scout Leader in a brief ceremony during a Troop Meeting. With the Patrols in a horse-shoe, the point should be made by the Scout Leader that the decision is that of the Patrol Leaders' Council, whilst the new Patrol Leader or Assistant Patrol Leader should be asked if he is prepared to accept the responsibility that the appointment carries. If possible, the Group Scout Leader should be present to add his good wishes and encouragement to that of the Scout Leader.

## No delay

One general point about the presentation of all awards for achievement is that there should be the minimum of delay between an award being gained and the ceremony in which the Scout receives the badge as tangible recognition of that achievement. Whilst in an ideal world it may be a good idea to wait for the Group Annual Meeting to take place so that other members may be there when a Chief Scout's Award is presented, another opportunity should be found to hold the ceremony if the Annual Meeting is more than a week or two away. There is no reason, of course, why

Scouts who have received the Chief Scout's Award should not come to the Annual Meeting so that reference can be made to what they have achieved, but once a badge or award has been agreed the Scout should receive this at the next available opportunity.

## Other occasions

Patrols and Troops will have their own traditions for other occasions which are not, strictly speaking, ceremonies but rather times when order is called for. It is helpful if Scouts know what is expected of them at these times and the following are suggestions for discussion by the Patrol Leaders' Council:

•**Inspection.** Should an inspection of uniform be held at the beginning of every Troop Meeting? Perhaps the Scout Leader and/or the Assistant Scout Leaders could inspect some weeks and the Patrol Leaders at other times. What happens in camp – do you have inspection every day in camp (above the knees), on alternate days or when you are going out from camp? What other things should be inspected at camp?

•**Notices.** Few things are guaranteed to bore everyone to tears more than a long tirade of notices given out by word of mouth at the end of an enjoyable (and tiring) Troop Meeting. Some general notices may be necessary, but where possible details of activities should be given to Scouts by their Patrol Leaders, supplemented from time to time with a typed sheet or newsletter so that parents have the chance to find out what is happening, too.

•**Uniform.** The Patrol Leaders' Council needs to decide when uniform is to be worn for Patrol and Troop Meetings, and every Scout should be aware of what has been decided. At Troop Meetings does everyone change into activity gear after Inspection and back into uniform again before closing ceremonies? Is it clearly understood that – for reasons of safety – uniform will not be suitable for adventurous activities? When uniform is worn, it should be smart and correct.

•**Call signs.** A simple and quiet sign to call everyone together can be a useful means of saving time. You may have a tradition of doing this (holding both arms out horizontally means that Patrols form up around your Headquarters, for example), but if not, find out what other Patrols and Troops do in your District – and then adopt or adapt those ideas for yourself.

•**Troop yells.** Some sort of yell or cheer at the end of a badge or award presentation ceremony is a way for the rest of the Troop to add their congratulations. A yell needs to be one of encouragement and enthusiasm. Again, if you don't have a tradition of these in your Troop, find out what others do and adopt or adapt . . . or work out your own.

Action 3

# Visits

Patrol visits to a place of interest locally are more worthwhile if they are linked in some way with training that Scouts are doing for one or other of the awards or for a Proficiency Badge. When arranging a visit, explain beforehand the requirements of an award or badge to those who are meeting or showing you around. Here are a few suggestions for visits:
Airport; art gallery; amateur radio station; ambulance station; bakery; castle; church or place of worship other than your own; cinema; club – for archery, fencing, gym, judo, shooting; dockyard; factory; fire station; gas works; harbour; historical site; local council meeting; magistrates' court; mine; meteorological station; motor repair garage; museum; newspaper offices; police station; post office; power station; printing works; sewage works; stables; telephone exchange; televison or radio studio; ten-pin bowling alley; theatre; zoo.

It might not be possible for all members of the Patrol to go on some visits – there may be minimum age limits and some will be of more interest to a group of older Scouts working on a particular project.

# People

Invite someone to come to a Patrol meeting or to meet a group of Scouts who are working on a particular topic together. Ask your visitor to talk about his work or hobby, explaining beforehand how he can help with the Scout Progressive Award Training Programme. Some ideas are:

**Animal welfare.** The local vet or someone from the nearest branch of the Royal Society for the Prevention of Cruelty to Animals.

**Fire service.** Find out how commercial premises are given advice on fire prevention, what fire precautions exist for blocks of flats in your area and how to deal with a fire at your home or in the Scout Headquarters.

**Home safety.** Your local council may have someone who can talk about this topic and suggest ways in which Scouts can help the elderly and those who live alone to identify possible dangers in their homes.

**Police.** Many areas now have home-beat policemen. Do you know the officer working in your area? Invite him to meet the Patrol – he may be able to suggest crime prevention and road safety officers who would come along later.

# Games

**Change handball**

You will need: a football; a piece of chalk.

Mark two chalk lines on the floor about 4m (13ft) apart. One Patrol stands on one chalk line and the opposing Patrol on the other line. Scouts link arms and defend their line with their feet, whilst one Scout from each Patrol tries to score a goal by shooting the ball over the other Patrol's line. When 'change' is called, the two Scouts in the field of play return to the left end of

their Patrol lines and are replaced by two Scouts from the right end of the Patrols.

**Pandemonium**

Define the playing area, either by marking it with chalk or with a circle of rope on the grass. One Patrol tries to sit on the ground, whilst the other Patrol attempts to stop them.

**The long reach**

Mark a chalk line down the centre of a hall or playground, with the Patrols on one side of the line. One Scout in each Patrol has a piece of chalk – the aim is for the Scouts with the chalk to mark an 'x' on the ground as far over the chalk line as possible, without touching the ground. The Scout with the chalk can be supported and helped by other members of the Patrol, none of whom may cross the line or touch the ground on the other side.

## Line-throwing

Practise line-throwing in the Patrol – it's useful in pioneering when you want to get a rope across an obstacle such as a stream and for rescue work. Use good quality braided line of about three-quarter inch circumference.

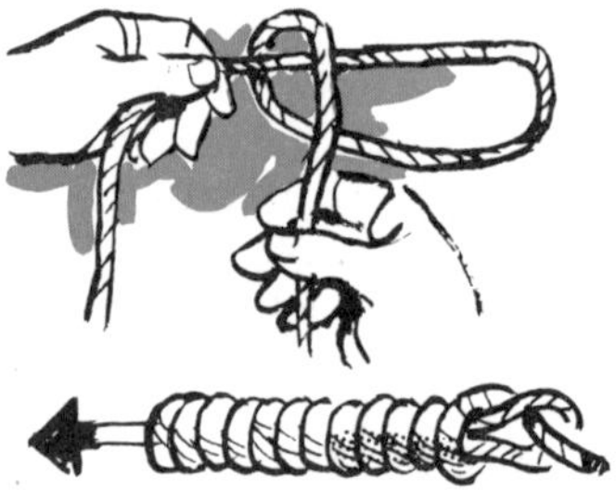

*For rescue work it's best to load one end of the line with the heaving-line knot. Take a bight in the line about $1\frac{1}{2}$m (5ft) from one end. Start frapping both parts of the bight, beginning about 20cm (8ins) from the end. Slip the tail through the small loop and tighten.*

*For line-throwing practice the monkey's fist will provide more weight. Start about 2m (6ft) from the end.*

*Everything depends on how you coil and handle the line before you throw it. Make a wrist loop and then lay the turns alongside each other without crossing, working towards the tips of the fingers and turning it so that the free end is nearest the fingertips. Without disturbing the turns, transfer two-thirds of the coil to the throwing hand.*

*Stand with the left shoulder towards the target area, swing both arms together across the body (under-arm) and throw with a good follow-through.*

# Activities for hikes

**Beeline hike**
The Patrol try to walk from point A to point B on a map – in a straight line. Provide tracing paper and pencil – and the route followed is marked. Of course they will have to take account of private property, railway lines, rivers and other dangers, but the line travelled should be as straight as possible.

**Hike out, ride back**
The Patrol hike to a point of interest some distance from your Headquarters and is met later in the day by one of the parents in a car. Provide the Patrol with the grid reference of the meeting point, but make sure that the parent driving the car knows exactly where the Patrol will be met.

**Heads or tails**
Try this in the town (with a street map) or in the country (with a large scale Ordnance Survey map). At the first junction in the road or footpath, the Patrol toss a coin; heads they go left and tails they turn right. The route taken can be marked on a tracing paper overlay so that it can be checked afterwards. After a set time limit, the Patrol make their way back to base by the shortest possible route.

**Compass walk**
Attach cards to a dozen widely scattered trees in an open area (use sticky tape and remove them after the activity). Each card gives the bearing and number of metres to the next marked tree. Working in pairs with a compass and setting out at two minute intervals, the Scouts are timed over the course.

**Homing pigeon hike**
Arrange for parents with cars to drop pairs of Scouts about five miles from your Headquarters. It is more fun if the Scouts are blindfolded during the car journey so that when they are dropped off the first thing they have to discover is where they are! Each pair has a map and compass – and the first pair back to the Headquarters wins.

**Nature memory hunt**
Before the hike commences, spread out about 20 items that can be found in the area the Patrol will be covering – an acorn, a bird's feather, leaves of trees and wild flowers, cones, wild berries and so on. The Patrol has two minutes to study the items. During the hike they collect as many of the same species as they were shown as possible. Impress on the Scouts that they must not uproot plants or disturb animals whilst looking for items.

**Listening hike**
Blindfold one or two members of the Patrol. Their job is to be led over the hike route by other Scouts in the Patrol and to listen to everything they hear along the way. Arrange for a number of incidents to occur along the route — a car that won't start, a conversation between two people in French, someone clipping a hedge in a garden or repairing a car.

# Rope ladders

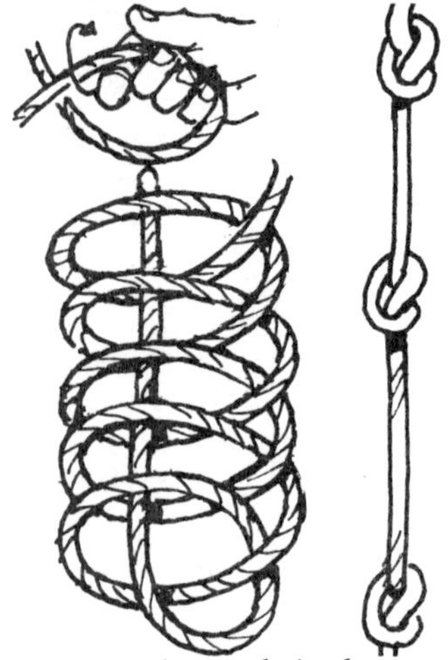

*To make a knotted single rope ladder, coil the length of rope into a series of half-hitches (by twisting the rope away from you), then pass the end of the rope right through the centre. Turn the coil inside out – and, holding one end, throw the coil away from you. As it pays out, a series of overhand or thumb knots are made along the rope – use these to support your feet as you climb up the rope.*

*Make a single rope ladder with chocks of hardwood about 15cm (6ins) diameter by about 5cm (2ins) deep, with holes bored in the centre to take the diameter of rope you are using. Either open the strands of rope beneath each block, insert small wooden pegs and bind them in or put two strands of seizing between the strands of the rope and then use a wall knot.*

*For the wooden rung ladder, lay two ropes out on the ground parallel to each other. Place the rungs across both sides at regular intervals and attach the ropes to each end of the rungs using the marline spike hitch. The ladder using poles with ropes for the lashings is a bush ladder. Start with a sheer lashing at the top and then open out the poles and lash the other poles across.*

Chapter 4

# The Patrol

If you are new to being a Patrol Leader you will have your own ideas about what the job involves. You have been a Scout in a Patrol and you have seen how other Patrol Leaders work. Sometimes you will have agreed with the way they set about things and at other times you may have felt that you would have done things in a different (and better?) way. Well, now you have the chance!

## The Patrol Leader's job

Here is a list of some of the things that you will be expected to do as a Patrol Leader. Read through the list and think about it first – for you may agree or disagree with some of the points we are making.

When you have thought it through, discuss the list with other Patrol Leaders, both those who are new and those with experience in leading their Patrols. Discuss the list, too, with your Assistant Patrol Leader and work out your priorities together. You will both have other commitments to your family, to your school and to the community and you will want to work as a team with each taking particular responsibilities within the Patrol and the Troop.

Take the opportunity as well to discuss your responsibilities and priorities with the Scouters, with your parents and with friends.

And here is our list, but remember that it is a list to which you may wish to add other things.

The Patrol Leader:

- **Sets** an example to others in his personal behaviour and his approach to life.
- **Makes** arrangements for Scouts to complete the Scout and Explorer Awards.
- **Helps** his Scouts to gain the Patrol Activity Award.
- **Plans** programmes for his Patrol, working with his Assistant Patrol Leader and Scouts in the Patrol to achieve this.
- **Plans** programmes for the Troop by working with other members of the Patrol Leaders' Council.
- **Puts** forward ideas for activities in the District and helps to organise them.
- **Finds** out what activities the Scouts in his Patrol would enjoy and carries these views forward to the Patrol Leaders' Council and the District.
- **Takes** a full part in the work of the Patrol Leaders' Council and accepts collective responsibility for the decisions that are made there.
- **Makes** sure that younger Scouts settle into the Patrol, feel welcome and enjoy their Scouting.
- **Helps** to maintain discipline.
- **Organises** Patrol meetings and other activities, involving members of the Patrol in running them.
- **Arranges** Patrol camps and helps to organise Troop camps, encouraging others in the Patrol to take part in the planning and to accept responsibility for some part of the organisation or programme.
- **Puts** the Patrol before himself.
- **Helps and supports** the Scout Leader in what he is trying to achieve for the Scout Troop.
- **Encourages** team spirit in his Patrol and within the Troop.
- **Completes** his own training

through the Scout Section Training Programme.

- **Accepts** responsibility – both personal responsibility for his own actions and collective responsibility for the decisions of the Patrol Leaders' Council.
- **Delegates** wherever possible to his Assistant Patrol Leader and to other Scouts in the Patrol – taking into account each Scout's abilities and training.

It is a long list and one that will spark off discussion that will help you (and others) to see your job as a Patrol Leader more clearly.

## Getting going

At the start your main job as a Patrol Leader will be in getting the members of your Patrol doing things that they enjoy and which they feel have a purpose. Just because you are interested in fishing does not mean that every member of your Patrol will dash out to buy a rod and line merely to please you!

Find out what training they want to do, where each Scout is in the training scheme and then talk through their ideas for activities. Start with activities that you can tackle and don't aim too high at first. Once you have run a successful activity that the Scouts in your Patrol have enjoyed, they will want more.

Sometimes the activity will be for all members of the Patrol and at others it will involve one or two Scouts working together. You will lead some activities and your Assistant Patrol Leader will look after others. Don't forget that the Scouters are there to help, too, and for some activities other adults who work with the Troop may be prepared to come along to offer training.

Everyone likes to feel that they are wanted and as the Patrol Leader it is up to you to involve the Scouts in your Patrol as much as possible in the planning and running of activities. Try to find out what each Scout is good at doing or enjoys – and then use his talents so that everyone in the Patrol benefits.

## Patrol organisation

One way to help Scouts to feel that they are wanted and involved is to ask everyone in the Patrol to take on a particular job. We are listing some of these jobs here. It is not an exhaustive list, nor do all the jobs have to be filled. In the summer when you may be camping more often, having someone to look after the equipment and food might be a good idea – and they will certainly have plenty to do. However, if you are not planning to go to camp in the winter, asking someone in the Patrol to plan menus for camps that are months away will seem a little pointless. It is far better to find another job that needs doing.

Change the jobs around from time to time and try whenever possible to ask a Scout to take on a job from which he will gain personal benefits. He may not always think he will enjoy doing that job, but if it helps him to make progress in the training scheme, explain this to him and encourage him to try.

Discuss the jobs that need to be done – first with your Assistant Patrol Leader and then with the rest of the Scouts in the Patrol. Don't merely tell people the jobs you want done – get them on your side and explain why someone has to take on these specific responsibilities within the Patrol.

## Assistant Patrol Leader

The position of Assistant Patrol Leader is not a 'job' in the way that some of the suggestions that follow are – rather it is an appointment made by the Patrol Leader with the approval of the Scout Leader and the Patrol Leaders' Council. It is not a job that can be moved around from time to time amongst other Scouts in the Patrol – although you will no doubt hope that one day your Assistant (who deputises for you when you cannot be present) will become a Patrol Leader himself. For this reason alone, you will want to give your Assistant responsibility not only to help you and the Patrol, but also to prepare him for further responsibility later on.

He is *your* Assistant and you have had a say in choosing him. Just assisting and being in the background all the time can be boring, so do encourage him to do things in his own right and not to live in your shadow.

Discuss with your Assistant any

special jobs that you would like him to take on or that he might suggest that he could tackle. If the Patrol is involved in a service project, your Assistant could be the Scout to lead it. If one or two Cub Scouts, or new entrants from outside the Group, are coming into the Patrol you may decide through discussion with your Assistant that he could either help them to settle down and make progress in the training scheme – or leave you to do that, whilst he looks after other activities for the older Scouts in the Patrol.

Help him to feel part of the running of the Troop – by suggesting that he might come to a Patrol Leaders' Council to see how things work there and by taking part in a Patrol Leaders' training course outside the Troop. When the Patrol Leaders' Council is planning training for Patrol Leaders within the Troop, suggest that Assistant Patrol Leaders might be included in all (or part) of the programme.

## Patrol Treasurer

The Patrol Leaders' Council is responsible for the Troop's funds, but if each Patrol has a Treasurer this can be a great help. He collects the subscriptions from members of the Patrol and hands them to the Troop's Treasurer. If part of the Troop subscription is allocated to Patrol funds, the Patrol Treasurer keeps an account of how much money comes in and how this is spent. The Troop or Group Treasurer will offer advice on a simple system for keeping track of the Patrol's money.

The Patrol Treasurer might be asked to collect money for the Patrol's activities and camps, to pay the bills and keep an account of how the money is spent.

Look through his account book with him and check the cash from time to time to show that you are interested. It's not a terribly exciting job, but it will make life easier for the Patrol Leader if someone in the Patrol is looking after the money.

## Patrol Quartermaster

The Patrol will need some equipment of its own for training (compass, maps, felt pens, paper, rope and so on) and it's best to have someone in the Patrol looking after it. Ideally each Patrol wants a place in the Group's Headquarters to store its equipment, but if this isn't possible the Patrol Quartermaster might keep things at home – but readily available for any training that needs to be done during the week or at weekends.

Keep a list of the Patrol's equipment and when new items are purchased, add these to the list.

Sometimes the Patrol will need to borrow equipment from the Group's store – pioneering gear for a day's activity at the local camp site, lifejackets if the Patrol is going canoeing, tentage for Patrol camps and so on. The Patrol Quartermaster is the Scout to make up the list of equipment you need, to arrange for its collection and return – and to report any damage or breakages.

Occasionally the Group Quartermaster will need help with repairing equipment and in getting it ready for camps and activities. The Patrol Quartermaster could offer to help and encourage others in the Patrol to lend a hand, too.

## Caterer

Food is often an important part of an activity – and it certainly is on a hike or at a camp. The Patrol Caterer prepares menus and food lists, arranges to buy the food and sorts out the cost with the Patrol Treasurer. But just because he buys the food, it does not follow that he has to do all the cooking when the Patrol is away at camp!

As with most things, it is a good idea to start off in a small way – with the Caterer getting the tea, milk, sugar and biscuits for a Patrol meeting – and to work up to the hikes and camps from there. Other things for the Caterer to do (especially in the winter months when he will not be at his busiest) are collecting recipes and arranging for practice sessions to try out some new ones – perhaps at home in a kitchen with mum on hand to keep an eye on things. The Patrol Caterer might help younger Scouts with their training in menu planning and cooking.

## Record-keeper

Each Scout keeps a record of his achievements in his *Scout Record Book*, but the Patrol may decide to have its own wall-chart and attendance register – and the Record-keeper makes sure that this is up to date.

A Patrol log book is a good idea – recording programmes of meetings, activities and camps, with photographs and drawings that are good to look back on in the years ahead. This could be kept by the Patrol Record-keeper, but other members of the Patrol should be encouraged to contribute to it as well. If you have a Group or Troop magazine or newsletter, the Record-keeper could make sure that the activities and achievements of the Patrol are written up and passed to the editor.

The job of Record-keeper will appeal to some Scouts, but not to others. If your Record-keeper clearly finds it boring, give him another job to do and ask someone else to take on the record-keeping for a while. Scouts rarely join because they want to write up reports or tap typewriter keys, and this is a job that should be moved around fairly often (unless you find someone who really does enjoy it).

## First Aider

Always take a first aid kit with you on any activity – with one or two bandages, plasters, safety pins, tweezers, antiseptic and the like. For a hike, camp or expedition you will need more things.

The Patrol First Aider makes sure that the necessary first aid items go with the Patrol. He might work with someone in the Group who helps with first aid training – an Assistant Scout Leader, Venture Scout or parent – and keep his supplies up to date with their advice. The Scout taking on this job does not need to be an expert first aider, but it is advisable to have someone in the Patrol who is and who can deal with emergencies when they arise.

# Patrol meetings

Here are just a few of the opportunities that members of the Patrol will have to meet together:

- **At Troop Meetings.** Whilst some of the activities, games and training sessions will involve your Patrol with the rest of the Troop, there will be time for the Patrols to meet together – for training and for planning activities in the days and weeks ahead.

•**At other times.** Hold Patrol meetings at other times. Don't meet for too long – an hour is long enough for the first one or two meetings – and decide what you are going to do before you get there. You will need to find an evening or a time at a weekend that suits most members of the Patrol. Where you meet will be up to you – you may be able to use your Scout Headquarters or meet in the homes of members of the Patrol. Make sure that Patrol meetings have a purpose – for training or just for fun.

There will be times when one or two members of the Patrol will want to meet together – the Patrol Quartermaster and Caterer when preparing for a Patrol camp, or two or three Scouts who are training for a Proficiency Badge.

•**Outings.** Find out the things that interest the Scouts in your Patrol and suggest an outing one evening, at a weekend or during the holidays. A visit to the swimming pool, to see a football match, to the cinema, for a bowling session – the list is endless. Take cost into account and if people are hard up, find something that won't take a lot of

pocket money – a visit to a museum, the fire or police station, a local nursery or whatever else is near where you live and where they don't make an entrance charge.

•**Hikes and expeditions.** A hike is a good way to get to know the other members of the Patrol (and it's a good idea to do this before you go away to camp for a few days). Involve all the members of your Patrol in the planning and walk as far as the youngest Scout can go without getting over-tired. Make it a half-day for the first hike and later take the whole day, cooking your lunch together.

Bring some variety into your hikes and expeditions – use public transport to travel to and from a part of the country you have not been to before, or take your cycles for a change.

Remember that the Patrol does not have to be together all the time – how about the older Scouts hiking a longer distance (with the Assistant Patrol Leader) whilst the younger Scouts explore the district nearer home (with you)?

•**Camps.** We will be talking more about camps in Chapter 9, but

Patrol camps are really extended Patrol meetings where you stay away from home overnight. Let everyone take part in the planning, for there is more chance that they will come if they have bought the food and helped to put the programme together.

Where you meet and what you do and when you do it – these are all things for you and your Patrol to decide. Keep your Scout Leader informed of what you are doing and if you are going to be away from home for the day or overnight, make sure that parents have all the details they need.

If you can find a place where the Patrol can meet that is yours and yours alone, you will be fortunate. A den for the Patrol is the ideal – but don't be put off if a den is not available, for few Patrols are lucky enough to have one. If you use the Scout Headquarters for Patrol meetings, clean up afterwards. If you meet in the homes of your Scouts, thank their parents and keep the noise down – and they might invite you back.

Above all, listen to the ideas your Scouts are putting forward for camps, activities and outings – and then do your best to make them work for everyone's benefit.

## The Patrol-in-Council

The Patrol-in-Council is an informal meeting of all Scouts in the Patrol. It is a good idea to have a Patrol-in-Council shortly before a Patrol Leaders' Council, so that you can seek the views of Scouts in the Patrol on things that are to be discussed (but remember to report back at the next Patrol-in-Council so that the Scouts know the outcome).

Keep the Patrol-in-Council short – and make sure it has a purpose. Decide what you want to talk about beforehand and make a list of the points – giving everyone in the Patrol a chance to contribute their points of view or to raise other matters. Make a note of what is decided and, if action is to be taken, who will do it.

Action 4

# Emergencies

With the help of Venture Scouts, parents and other adults in the Group, arrange a series of emergency incidents – one for each Patrol to tackle in turn.

Make the incidents as realistic as possible, using plastic wounds and make-up. Find out if there are any Venture Scouts or members of the first aid organisations locally who specialise in casualty simulation for this kind of exercise and ask for help.

If the incidents are in a place where the public will see them, advise the police beforehand so that they know what you are doing and put up a notice stating that this is a training exercise – otherwise a member of the public may ring for the emergency services.

When you have decided on the incidents you will stage, ask an expert in first aid and emergencies to assist you both in setting the scene and in noting down the actions that should be taken in order. At each incident have a Venture Scout or other adult watching how the Patrols tackle things, so that they can comment afterwards.

**Car crash**
A car has taken a bend in the road too sharply, mounted the grass verge and hit a tree. The driver is slumped over the wheel and a passenger is lying in the road. The car engine is still running.

**Rope**
A Scout on an obstacle course has slid down a rope some 7m (21ft), suffering friction burns to his hands and arms, and spraining his ankle on landing. He is unconscious when the Patrol arrive on the scene.

**Group stores**
A Scout is packing tentage away in the Group stores after a weekend camp. He trips over a tent on the ground and catches his arm on a bread knife, gashing the arm badly. He is found on the ground, unconscious and in a pool of blood.

**Mechanic**
A Venture Scout has removed the radiator cap in his car inside his garage at home. The radiator was boiling and the engine running. Scalding water has splashed onto his arm and, in the confusion, he put his other hand into the fan, lacerating his fingers. He is conscious but complaining.

**Others**
- A boy has fallen over a bridge onto a tow path.
- A Scout has been struck by lightning.
- A small girl has been hit by a falling tree branch and is unconscious.
- Injuries in the home – falling down stairs, falling from a window, electrocution by a defective flex, burning from a chip pan fire.
- Injuries in the Group Headquarters – splinters in the hands, cuts from glass.

# Leathercraft

**Raw materials**

Craft shops sell leather off-cuts of various shapes and sizes. If you don't have a craft shop nearby, ask your local shoe repairer for advice on a source of supply. Use pieces cut from old plastic handbags (obtained from jumble sales) for practice.

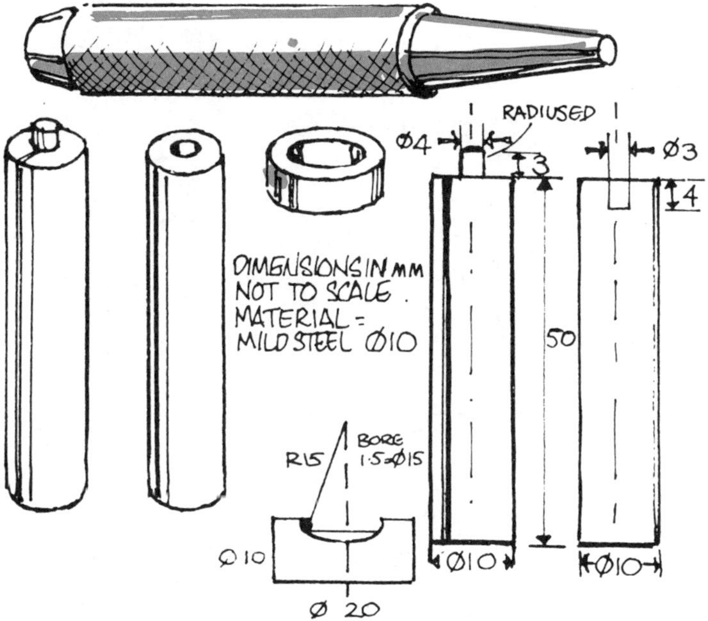


*The leather punch (above top) is for making holes in the leather to fit press studs. You will need to buy the press stud parts, but the tools could be made by a member of the Patrol.*

**Tools**

You will need: a pair of sharp scissors (which are best for cutting thin leather and the safest); a sharp cutting knife (for thicker leather and for shapes and slots); a steel rule or straight edge; a cutting board; a punch or nail and hammer (for making holes in the leather for fitting press studs and for thonging – joining leather using thin strips or thongs of leather); press stud tools and press studs (which can be bought in craft shops); pliers.

*To make a flat leather woggle, mark out the shape on the reverse side of the piece of leather and cut with scissors. Punch two press stud holes and then fit the press studs as shown. Heat a metal object, holding it in the pliers and brand the shape onto the leather – use a hot nail to write letters or to pierce holes.*

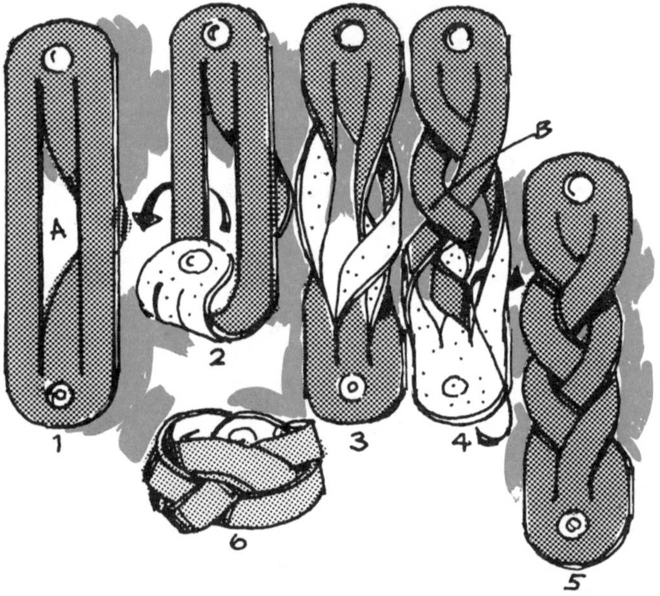


*To make a plaited woggle, cut the slots with a sharp knife and straight edge before cutting the outline with scissors – it will be easier to keep still. Fit the press studs. Pull the centre strand to the right as in (1) and lift the lower end and thread it through the left-hand gap at 'A' as in (2). Pull the threaded end straight as in (3). Starting at the top, plait each strand to lie over and under each other as shown in (5). When the upper plaits are crossed and flattened to the point where the centre crosses the right at 'B', the lower end will twist up forwards. It may then be threaded right through the right-hand gap as shown at (4). It is then only necessary to turn all the strands topside up.*

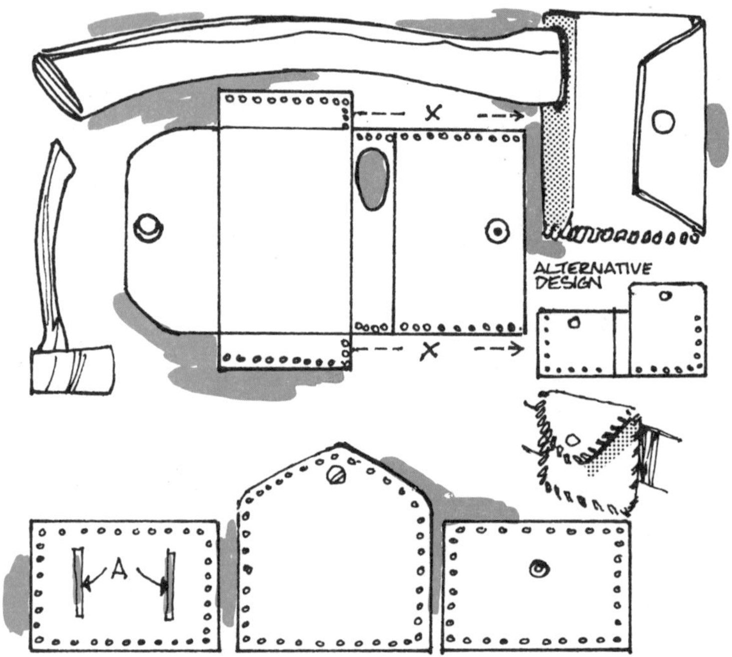


*With more complex shapes such as this axe sheath or belt purse, it's probably best to make a paper pattern first – then you will know if the shape is correct before cutting into the leather. The sides can be sewn if the leather is not too thick, using a sharp needle and strong thread. Thonging is more attractive. Mark out on the reverse side the line of holes and then make them with the punch. Use thin leather thongs to join the edges together. Remember when making the belt purse to cut the slots, marked at 'A', to allow your belt to be threaded through when the purse is completed.*

Chapter 5

# Training in the Troop

The Scout Section Training Programme is an integrated scheme incorporating training activities, awards, the Proficiency Badge Scheme and the Patrol System, with a series of awards and badges to mark achievement and progress. Much of the training will be carried out in Patrol and Troop activities – at meetings, on expeditions and in camp. There are basic skills to be learned (to help a Scout to look after himself) and a wide range of other interests (to extend a Scout's knowledge and to help him to be of service to others).

However, training is not just for Scouts – Patrol Leaders and Scouters need to train for their jobs, too. But first we will look at opportunities that are available to Scouts in the Troop.

## The Scout Section Training Programme

It is important to recognise that the Scout Section Training Programme is part of an overall progressive scheme that starts in the Cub Scout Pack and follows through to the Venture Scout Unit – and the diagram on page 50 shows how this progression works through a series of related activity areas.

Cub Scouts acquire skills and experience which are of value when they move to the Troop, where that experience is widened and extended. Scouts use those skills in a range of activities and when they move to the Venture Scout Unit they will continue to find opportunities – both in adventurous activities and in service to others. The programme links the Pack, Troop and Unit so that each is not isolated from the other, offering progressive achievement through activities rather than a series of hurdles to be jumped and tested.

### Main features

The main features of the Scout Section Training Programme are:

• **Badges.** There is a Scout Membership Badge; four progressive training awards – the Scout Award ($10\frac{1}{2}$–$11\frac{1}{2}$), Pathfinder Award ($11\frac{1}{2}$–13), Explorer Award (13–14) and Chief Scout's Award (14–$15\frac{1}{2}$); in addition there are the Patrol Activity Award ($10\frac{1}{2}$–$15\frac{1}{2}$), the Leadership Award (13–$15\frac{1}{2}$) and the Chief Scout's Challenge (14–$15\frac{1}{2}$), plus a wide range of Proficiency Badges.

• **Younger and older Scout.** The content of the Scout Award and the Pathfinder Award are aimed at the younger Scout of $10\frac{1}{2}$ to 13, whilst the Explorer Award and the Chief Scout's Award have a range of activities that are suited to the older Scout aged 13 to $15\frac{1}{2}$.

# Relationship between Cub Scout, Scout and Venture Scout programmes

<table>
<tr><th colspan="3">Cub Scouts</th><th colspan="4">Scouts</th><th colspan="2">Venture Scouts</th></tr>
<tr><th>Bronze Arrow</th><th>Silver Arrow</th><th>Gold Arrow</th><th>10½–11½<br>Scout Award</th><th>11½–13<br>Pathfinder Award</th><th>13–14<br>Explorer Award</th><th>14–15½<br>Chief Scout's Award</th><th>Venture Award</th><th>Queen's Scout Award</th></tr>
<tr><td colspan="3" rowspan="2">Growing up</td><td colspan="4">Health</td><td>Physical Activities</td><td rowspan="2">Pursuits/ Interests</td></tr>
<tr><td colspan="4">Scoutcraft</td><td>Creative Pursuits</td></tr>
<tr><td colspan="3" rowspan="2">Discovering</td><td colspan="4">Adventure</td><td>Outdoors and Environment</td><td rowspan="2">Exploration</td></tr>
<tr><td colspan="4">Culture</td><td>International Dimension</td></tr>
<tr><td colspan="3" rowspan="2">Thinking</td><td colspan="4">Commitment</td><td>Design for Living</td><td rowspan="2">Commitment</td></tr>
<tr><td colspan="4">Leadership</td><td>Personal Values</td></tr>
<tr><td colspan="3" rowspan="2">Sharing</td><td colspan="4">The Patrol</td><td>Relationships</td><td rowspan="2">Community</td></tr>
<tr><td colspan="4">Community</td><td>Community</td></tr>
<tr><td colspan="3">Proficiency Badges</td><td colspan="3">Proficiency Badges</td><td colspan="3">Duke of Edinburgh's Award Scheme</td></tr>
</table>

**•Direct entry.** A new entrant to the Scout Troop from outside the Movement first gains his Scout Membership Badge and then moves on to a point in the training programme that is appropriate to his age. Someone joining the Troop at thirteen would, therefore, not tackle the Scout Award or the Pathfinder Award, but start working straight away for the Explorer Award, whilst a fourteen-year-old would go straight into the Chief Scout's Award.

**•Moving direct.** If a Scout does not make progress relevant to his age, he may move direct to a more senior Award. Thus, a Scout who reaches his thirteenth birthday and who has not completed his Pathfinder Award (which is for the 11½- to 13-year-old) may move straight on to the Explorer Award (which is for the 13- to 14-year-old).

**•Water and Air Activities.** These are incorporated in the programme to support Sea and Air Scout Troops and, at the same time, to encourage these activities in other Scout Troops. These activities can also be found in the specialist four-staged Proficiency Badges, together with

more technical requirements for those wishing to pursue these subjects at a higher level. Each stage can count as the Proficiency Badge requirement for the appropriate Progressive Training Awards.

**•Compulsory activities.** Because every Scout needs to learn a number of basic skills to enjoy Scouting to the full, the training activities in the Scout Award (the first award for the younger Scout) and the Explorer Award (the first award for the older Scout) are compulsory. In addition, Scouts coming into the Troop from outside the Movement and tackling the Pathfinder Award or the Chief Scout's Award have to complete certain compulsory items.

**•Choice.** A number of options, grouped according to subject and age, will be found in the detailed requirements of the training programme. Each set concludes with the words 'or any other one activity of a similar nature and level of achievement as agreed with the Patrol Leaders' Council'. This avoids long lists of options and it also means that Scouts can undertake other activities that they wish to try or which are available in their home area. It also places responsibility on the Patrol Leaders' Council to ensure that the activity is a similar one and that the level of achievement required is similar, too. It may not always be possible for all the options shown to be available to the Scout and this is an opportunity for decisions to be made by the Scout and the Patrol Leaders' Council on which of the options are practicable for their Troop.

• **Programme balance.** The detailed requirements of each award are balanced, not only to ensure that the activities are within the capabilities of the age groups, but also to give more emphasis to Scoutcraft for the younger Scout and with the accent on adventure for the older Scout.

• **Scouts with a handicap.** Handicapped Scouts should be encouraged to undertake all activities in the programme, but certain of these may need to be modified in consultation with the Scout, the Patrol Leaders' Council and, possibly, the Assistant District Commissioner (Handicapped), parents and others. If a compulsory activity is plainly impossible because of a Scout's particular handicap, an alternative from the appropriate option lists of either the Pathfinder or the Chief Scout's Award may be substituted.

Direct entry Scouts who are known to be slow-learners may start on the award appropriate to their ability or to their age – in which case certain activities may need to be modified. For example, a slow-learning 13½-year-old may take the Scout Award, the Pathfinder Award or the Explorer Award. The decision as to which award he should take would be made after discussion with the Scout, the Patrol Leaders' Council, the Assistant District Commissioner (Handicapped) and the Scout's parents.

## Details of the programme

Full details of the award requirements will be found in *Policy, Organisation and Rules*. The requirements for all the Proficiency Badges, including the four Airmanship and Seamanship stages, are in *Scout Proficiency Badges*. Every Scout should have his own copy of the *Scout Record Book,* which is pocket-sized and contains an outline of the training programme and a checklist so that a Scout may mark off his progress as items are completed.

We would hope that every Scout would also have his own copy of the book for the award on which he is working. The two books are *The Fun of Scouting* (for the younger Scout, covering the Scout Membership Badge, Scout Award, Pathfinder Award and Patrol Activity Award) and *Challenge and Adventure* (for the older Scout, covering the Scout Membership Badge, Explorer Award, Chief Scout's Award, Patrol Activity Award, Leadership Award and Chief Scout's Challenge).

The following notes, which should be read in conjunction with the detailed requirements, cover points that will be of particular interest to Patrol Leaders, Scout Leaders and the Patrol Leaders' Council in operating the scheme within their Patrols and Troop.

• **Link Badge.** This is not, strictly speaking, part of the Scout Section

Training Programme for it is taken by a Cub Scout during his last few months in the Pack, but the Scout Leader and the Patrol Leaders' Council have a major part to play.

Firstly, it is passed under arrangements made jointly by the Cub Scout Leader, the Scout Leader and the Patrol Leaders' Council. Secondly, the Cub Scout has to talk with his future Patrol Leader about coming into the Troop, and with his Scout Leader about the meaning of the Scout Promise and Law. The Cub Scout takes part in a Patrol activity and a Troop Meeting, and learns something about the Scout Movement.

We have talked earlier in this book about helping Cub Scouts to settle into the Patrol and Troop – and working through the Link Badge requirements is part of this.

•**Scout Membership Badge.** This is passed under arrangements made jointly by the Scout Leader and the Patrol Leader, and awarded by the Patrol Leaders' Council.

A Scout who completed the Link Badge as a Cub Scout automatically gains this badge on making the Scout Promise as the requirements are exactly the same. The Scout Membership Badge is intended for those who join the Troop direct and have not moved up from a Cub Scout Pack. It must be completed before a Scout moves on to the next award appropriate to his age.

The purpose of the Scout Membership Badge is to help a new Scout to settle down in his Patrol and in the Troop. He takes part in a Patrol activity and a Troop Meeting, talks with his Patrol Leader about coming into the Troop, and learns something about the Scout Movement. He understands and accepts the Scout Promise and Law, and talks about their meaning with the Scout Leader.

•**Scout Award.** This is for Scouts of $10\frac{1}{2}$ to $11\frac{1}{2}$, and is passed under arrangements made by a Patrol Leader and awarded by the Patrol Leaders' Council.

There are four parts. The Scout must hold the Scout Membership Badge. He must complete successfully a series of compulsory training activities under the headings Scoutcraft, Adventure, Culture, Community, Health and Commitment. These headings occur again in later awards (as shown in the diagram on page 50) and in the Scout Award they cover basic skills that are needed to enjoy many Scout activities in safety. A Scout also takes part in two activities from the Patrol Activity Award and gains one Proficiency Badge.

•**Pathfinder Award.** This is for Scouts of $11\frac{1}{2}$ to 13, and is passed under arrangements agreed by the Scout Leader and awarded by the Patrol Leaders' Council. To start on this award the Scout must be $11\frac{1}{2}$ and hold the Scout Membership Badge *or* hold the Scout Award. A direct entrant coming into the Troop after he is 11 and starting straight away on the Pathfinder Award must also complete the Scoutcraft and Commitment activities from the Scout Award – in this way he will learn basic skills.

Scouts select twelve items from a list of training activities under the headings Scoutcraft, Adventure and so on, take part in two activities from the Patrol Activity Award and gain a Proficiency Badge (which must be a different one from that undertaken for the Scout Award).

•**Explorer Award.** This is for Scouts of 13 to 14, and is passed under arrangements made by a Patrol Leader and awarded by the Patrol Leaders' Council. The Scout must be at least 13 and hold the Scout Membership Badge *or* hold the Pathfinder Award.

A series of training activities (mostly compulsory and, again, under the headings Scoutcraft, Adventure and so on) are undertaken to ensure that the Scout gains a high level of essential skills. For this reason a direct entrant of 13 years is not required to complete parts of an earlier award to acquire basic skills. The Scout also has to gain two items from the Leadership Award and a further Proficiency Badge.

•**Chief Scout's Award.** This is for Scouts of 14 to $15\frac{1}{2}$, and is passed under arrangements agreed by the Scout Leader and awarded by the Patrol Leaders' Council. A direct entrant coming into the Troop after he is 14 and starting straight on the Chief Scout's Award must also complete the Scoutcraft and Commitment activities from the Explorer Award to be certain that he gains a higher level of essential skills. To start on this award a Scout must be at least 14 and hold the Scout Membership Badge *or* hold the Explorer Award.

Scouts select a series of twelve training activities under the headings Scoutcraft, Adventure, and so on and complete two items from the Leadership Award. In addition a further Proficiency Badge must be gained and finally the Scout must complete a personal project agreed with the Patrol Leaders' Council – this could be as a Cub Scout Instructor, gaining an Instructor Proficiency Badge and using it, completing the Chief Scout's Challenge, a project in another country, etc.

•**Patrol Activity Award.** This is for Scouts to tackle at any time in the Troop and is passed under arrangements made by the Patrol Leader and awarded by the Patrol Leaders' Council.

The requirements of the Patrol Activity Award may be passed at the same time as those for the Progressive Training Awards, for this will encourage a Scout to take part in training activities with other members of his Patrol. To reinforce this some of the requirements of the Patrol Activity Award will also be found in the Scout Award and the Pathfinder Award – and all of these involve Scouts taking part in Patrol-based activities. Having gained some of the requirements as part of the Scout Award and/or the Pathfinder Award, a Scout can – with a little extra effort – go on to gain the Patrol Activity Award in its own right.

Almost inevitably, the question will be asked at some time about what constitutes a 'Patrol activity'. For the purpose of the Patrol Activity Award, a Patrol activity is defined as one that is undertaken by at least four members of the same Patrol, working as a Patrol, that is the Patrol Leader with three Scouts; the Patrol Leader, the Assistant Patrol Leader and two Scouts; or four Scouts.

•**Leadership Award.** This is for older Scouts of 13 upwards. It offers them the opportunity for leadership and responsibility – and not just as Patrol Leaders and Assistant Patrol Leaders. To encourage this, some of the requirements of the Leadership Award will also be found in the Explorer Award and the Chief Scout's Award. Again, having completed some of the requirements as part of those two awards, a Scout can go on to gain the Leadership Award in its own right.

The Leadership Award offers responsibility and leadership within the Troop for all Scouts who are 13 and over – and not only for those older Scouts who are Patrol Leaders and Assistant Patrol Leaders.

•**Duke of Edinburgh's Award Scheme.** With planning the Duke of Edinburgh's Award Scheme can be run simultaneously with the Scout Section Training Programme.

•**Chief Scout's Challenge.** The Challenge is open to Scouts of 14 and above, and helps them to gain skills, to develop physically and to work together as a team. It is carried out under arrangements agreed by the Scout Leader with the Assistant

District Commissioner (Scouts) and awarded by the Patrol Leaders' Council in consultation with the Assistant District Commissioner (Scouts).

The Challenge falls into three parts. First, there is a training programme to be undertaken. Second, an expedition with a project is planned and carried out. Finally, the team reports back to the Troop.

- **Proficiency Badges.** These fall into five groups:
  - **Interest:** These are intended for younger Scouts in their first year or two in the Troop. Many younger Scouts will be developing hobbies and interests covered by these Proficiency Badges – and should be encouraged to take the appropriate Interest Badge in their early days in the Troop.
  - **Pursuit:** These are more challenging and require a Scout to explore a subject in greater depth. They are open to all Scouts, but intended more for those of 13 and over. Scouts should be encouraged to develop a new interest or to extend their knowledge of a subject through the Pursuit Proficiency Badges.
  - **Service:** Involving both theory and practice, these badges are open to all Scouts, but are intended for those who are older and are able to use their skills in helping others.
  - **Instructor:** These involve the theory and practice of instruction and are, again, intended for older Scouts. Instructor Badges may be acquired by those who hold the appropriate Interest, Pursuit, Service or Collective Achievement Badges. No more than two Instructor Badges may be held.
  - **Collective Achievement:** These are to encourage a Scout Patrol or a group of Scouts to work together on a project. The standard and duration of the project is decided by the Patrol Leaders' Council in discussion with those who are taking the badge.

Proficiency Badges are gained under arrangements made by the Scout Leader in consultation with the Group Scout Leader. The District Executive Committee may appoint examiners to supplement Troop arrangements.

Instructor Badges are passed under arrangements made by an examiner appointed by the District Executive Committee.

Collective Achievement Badges are awarded by the Patrol Leaders' Council, which will assess the project for progress, perseverance and achievement by the Patrol or group of Scouts.

- **Venture Scout Membership Badge and Venture Award.** A Scout may work and qualify for the Venture Scout Membership Badge and may meet requirements for the Venture Award during the three months prior to his transfer to the Unit.

## Standards

Ability in particular skills will vary from Scout to Scout. When assessing standards Patrol Leaders, Scout Leaders and the Patrol Leaders' Council will be looking for individual achievement and progress – we cannot expect that every Scout will match up with a set standard of attainment.

The books *The Fun of Scouting* and *Challenge and Adventure* will help to show the members of the Patrol Leaders' Council the minimum standards that should be achieved,

but standards have to be set for each individual Scout and not for everyone. Scouts should be encouraged to discuss their progress and the standards they are trying to achieve with the Patrol Leaders' Council.

## Patrol Leader Training

Training to be a Patrol Leader is something that is going on all the time – and it is not merely something you take part in over a weekend course. It starts when a Scout joins the Troop, as he watches how his Patrol Leader sets about the job – and it goes on from there.

The best Patrol Leader training takes place in the Scout Troop – through regular sessions which the Scout Leader and the Patrol Leaders have together, as well as through doing the work of a Patrol Leader and learning through experience and mistakes.

The Patrol Leaders and Scout Leader need to give time to this. A few minutes together after one night's Troop Meeting will provide the opportunity to arrange the detail of the programme for the next week. Sometimes it will be necessary to meet at another time – to discuss activities at Patrol meetings and the part that Patrol Leaders will play in Troop Meetings, camps and other activities. Don't be too ambitious at the start. Have short, informal discussions and training sessions and once you have had some successes, everyone will see the purpose and find that they are worthwhile.

Meetings of the Patrol Leaders' Council include discussion of matters affecting the Troop, but time must be allowed for planning programmes, too. As Patrol Leaders will be taking a leading part in running these programmes, they will need training not only in leadership skills, but in the practical skills involved as well. Anyone instructing or leading an activity needs to be at least two steps ahead of those who are learning – and it is essential that Patrol Leaders should receive adequate training beforehand.

In addition to the training that goes on week by week, some provision should be made for the Patrol Leaders to take part in evenings, days or weekends when the aim is to improve their skills in leadership and to take their own training a stage further. Whilst some of these sessions will be for Patrol Leaders only, it is a good idea to include Assistant Patrol Leaders and older Scouts from time to time. For some it will be training for the day when they are appointed as Patrol Leaders; for others it might be their only chance to take part in this kind of training, for every Scout does not necessarily have the opportunity to be a Patrol Leader.

Here are some suggestions for Patrol Leaders' training sessions to supplement what is being done in the Troop week by week:

•**Patrol Leaders' Council weekend.** The Patrol Leaders and Scout Leader go away for a weekend's training together. Decide beforehand on the skills that need to be practised and involve other adults to help with these – Assistant Scout Leaders, Venture Scouts, members of the District Scout Fellowship and so on.

•**With Patrol Leaders from another Troop.** There is much to be learned from finding out how other Patrols and Troops work. Invite the Patrol

Leaders from another Troop to join you for an evening, a day or a weekend. Work out the programme together beforehand.

•**In the District or County.** Courses over evenings or a weekend with Patrol Leaders and Scouters from other Troops in the area will broaden outlook and bring a breath of fresh air into your Patrols and Troop as you find out how others work. The programme of activities and training needs to be relevant to what the Patrol Leaders and Scouters are doing back in their own Troops week by week – concentrating on learning skills, how to instruct, assessing standards of achievement and so on. There is a place for a weekend of adventurous activities that will stretch the Patrol Leader and give him activity amongst those of his own age, but there is a difference between an activity weekend (in which a Patrol Leader makes personal progress) and a Patrol Leaders' training course (where he should make personal progress, but where other skills that will help him with his Patrol and in the Troop are acquired).

Patrol Leaders' training courses in which the Patrol Leaders work side by side with their Scout Leaders mean that when they are back in their own Troops both Patrol Leaders and Scout Leaders will have a common experience to draw on. If

Patrol Leaders attend a course on their own – and their Scout Leader is not part of this – there can be a tendency for the Patrol Leaders to find that their new-found enthusiasm is not necessarily shared by their Scout Leader. It is far better if they take part in the course together.

From time to time it is worthwhile inviting Assistant Patrol Leaders and older Scouts to take part in a course of this nature – for they both benefit personally and contribute to the course as well. Joint training with Girl Guide Patrol Leaders helps both Movements to learn from each other.

## Scout Leader Training

For Scout Leaders, too, training is going on all the time – in the Troop and in the Scout Group. It is there, too, at District Scouters' Meetings, which should not merely be talking-shops, but provide training opportunities for Leaders to widen their range of interest and expertise. Organisations outside Scouting can offer training for Leaders that will give a new dimension to what they in turn provide for the Troop in the week by week programme.

Within The Scout Association there is a formal training scheme for Leaders. The intention is to provide training support as quickly after appointment as possible and that training is practical and related to the job that the Leader is currently doing in Scouting.

There are three stages of training – Initial Training, Basic Training and Advanced Training. Scout Leaders – and other Section Leaders – are required to take all three parts. Assistant Leaders are expected to take Initial and Basic Training, and are encouraged to go on to take Advanced Training as well (although this is not obligatory).

- **Initial Training.** This takes place within three months of appointment as a Leader. Before appointment the potential Leader meets with the District Commissioner and goes to the District Appointments sub-Committee.

A personal training adviser is appointed to assist the new Scouter with his Initial Training, which consists of tasks which are carried out under the guidance and support of the personal training adviser.

- **Basic Training.** The aim is to complete this within a year of appointment as a Scouter. It consists of a 22-hour course, usually held over two short weekends. There are a series of obligatory subjects and the rest consists of optional subjects. There are different courses for each Section – and Scouters in the Scout Section are expected to spend one of the weekends in camp.

Each Leader is given a series of assignments to carry out in his own Scout Group before completion of the course.

- **Advanced Training.** This 40-hour course is completed by Section Leaders within five years of appointment. It may be held over a week, or over two long weekends and one evening, or sometimes over three weekends. There are some obligatory subjects whilst others are optional.

There is a different course for each Section, but sometimes courses are joint for certain parts of the training. Leaders have a number of assignments to carry out within their own Scout Groups.

Chapter 6

# The Patrol Leader and training in the Patrol

By far the best way to learn something new is by taking part in an activity. Scouts don't join to sit on the floor with bits of string learning how to tie knots – they come into your Patrol because they expect to climb trees, swing over ditches and build bridges across rivers. Learning to tie knots for the sake of it is hardly fun. Making a rope swing can be just that – and the fact that you have to learn the correct knots and lashings as you do so is a bonus.

Scouts expect that many of their activities will be out of doors. This will not always be possible and some training will have to take place in a hall or in one of your homes, but when a new skill has been learned indoors, try to find the earliest opportunity to enjoy an activity in the open air using that skill.

In the Scout Award there is a simple navigation exercise involving map and compass. Some of the training for this can be tackled indoors – learning how to set a map and about conventional signs, making contour models, working out scales and distances – but use a map of your home area and go outdoors as soon as possible to check what you have learned on the ground.

## Visual aids

Visual aids can add variety and help to make sure that the principles of a new skill are understood, but use the real thing whenever possible. There's little to be gained from spending time making a cardboard axe when a real hand-axe is available (although for safety's sake, make sure it has a leather mask fitted when it's not in use for chopping wood). Similarly, messing about with bits of string on the back of a chair is nowhere near as exciting as using ropes and spars.

Visual aids are often best if home-made and here are some you might try:

- **Charts:** The range of SCOUTING Magazine charts and those produced by other publishers give basic information which needs to be learned (and there are details in the reference pages at the back of this book of where these may be obtained).

•**Flip charts.** All you need to make a flip chart are some large sheets of paper clipped to a piece of thick card or plywood. Use felt tipped pens to write with. Cut out pictures from magazines and from old charts to illustrate the subject. Encourage members of the Patrol to draw their own flip chart material.

•**Flannel boards.** Stretch a piece of flannel material tightly across a sheet of plywood. Cut out pictures from magazines and old charts, and write any words you need on stiff card. Glue a piece of similar flannel to the backs of the pictures or pieces of card – and these will adhere to the flannel on the board. You can move the pieces about over the flannel board – and this is particularly useful for activities such as naming the parts of an axe, planning a Patrol camp site, and word games or puzzles. Everyone in the group can see what's happening and take part.

•**Films, videos and slides.** Libraries and specialist publishers are a source for these. Someone in the Patrol may have a projector or video on which they can be shown at a Patrol meeting (and if two or three Patrols arrange their meetings on the same or following nights, a number can share from one hiring). Slides or videos made at camp and on training activities can be used in the winter months to show how skills learned indoors can become exciting activities outside in the better weather.

•**Models.** Use models for training (of a Patrol camp site, for example), but don't leave it there. Go on and build that camp site for real and don't expect adventure to be gained from just modelling, enjoyable as it may be as an activity in itself.

•**Books and magazines.** These are visual aids in themselves (and, again, the reference pages give you some ideas). Use them to take the Patrol outdoors for the activity they came into the Patrol to enjoy.

## You can't be . . .

You can't expect to be an expert in everything and if your Patrol is going to enjoy a wide range of activities, you will need help from other leaders. And there's nothing to be ashamed of about this.

As a Patrol Leader you may be good at pioneering or canoeing, but not so keen (or expert) on first aid or navigation. That need not worry you for whilst you need to know something about a lot of subjects, you don't necessarily have to teach them all. There will be other leaders who would be grateful for your help with the topics you enjoy teaching, whilst they look after the skills at which they excel.

Look around amongst the other Patrol Leaders and the Assistant Patrol Leaders – but don't stop there. Older Scouts who may not be Patrol Leaders or Assistant Patrol Leaders would often welcome the chance to help – if asked.

Venture Scouts, parents, Scouters, members of the Scout Fellowship – there are plenty of people who may be able to help you to give your Patrol better training.

When you are planning a training activity, make sure that it is within the capabilities of the Scouts who are taking part and those who are leading. A young Scout, fresh from the Pack and keen to try everything, may want to go on a 20-mile hike after a month or so in your Patrol, but you need to decide if he has the training and the stamina to keep up with the others who are more experienced. Don't put him off or make him feel small or inadequate, but find a way for him to tackle something shorter and within his ability to enjoy.

Don't talk over the heads of your Scouts just because you like a subject and consider yourself something of an expert. Take things stage by stage to gain their interest and they may become as enthusiastic as you are.

Similarly, avoid teaching Scouts something they already know. Just because one or two younger Scouts need to learn about conventional signs does not mean that the older Scouts in your Patrol have to cover the same familiar ground yet again. Indeed, perhaps one of those older Scouts could do the teaching – leaving you free to tackle something else.

## Who takes part?

Sometimes all the members of the Patrol will enjoy a training activity together. At other times it will be one or two Scouts or an individual on his own. Occasionally there may be a number of Scouts from different Patrols.

Your Patrol might be out on a hike, cooking lunch together, but only the younger Scouts are preparing their meal for an award. The other members of the Patrol could be working towards a Proficiency Badge – or just cooking because they are hungry!

# How to train

There are three parts to any training activity – explaining, practising and following-up. If you are helping a young Scout to pack his rucsac, go through each of the steps and not only will he understand what he is doing and why he is doing it, but there is a better chance that he will keep what you are teaching him in his mind for the next time he packs his rucsac before a camp or expedition.

Taking a training activity like packing a rucsac, here's how the steps work:

• *Explain:* first, *tell* the Scout why he needs to learn how to pack his rucsac; then *demonstrate* how it's done.

• *Practise:* let the Scout *try it* for himself. When he has done so, *go over* what he has done and *show* him if there is a better way, explaining why you think this is so, but listening to (and perhaps accepting) his reasons for doing it differently. *Encourage* him to practise on his own during the week.

• *Follow-up:* make sure that the Scout *understands* what he has learned (and if it is an activity where safety is involved, that he really does appreciate the need to take extra care). Now that the Scout has learned how to pack his rucsac, *ask* him how this will help him to enjoy his Scouting more (knowing how to pack a rucsac leads on to camping, learning a new lashing means that he can try out his skill in a pioneering project – the point to get across is that each new skill learned gives him the chance to take part in more activities).

# Before you start

Here is a checklist of things to ask yourself as a Patrol Leader before any training activity:

• **What are we trying to do?** Learn a new skill, practise a skill we have learned already, enjoy an activity putting that skill into action.

• **Why are we doing this?** To complete part of the Scout Section Training Programme, to prepare for a Patrol activity, competition, camp or expedition.

• **Who will take part?** One or two Scouts in the Patrol, Cub Scouts working on the Link Badge, all the Patrol, other Scouts in the Troop.

• **Who will instruct?** You, your Assistant Patrol Leader, another Patrol Leader, someone else.

• **Where will you run the training?** In your Group's Headquarters, at the local camp site, in one of your homes, on a hike, in camp, somewhere else.

• **When?** On Troop Night, at a Patrol meeting, during a camp, at another time.

• **How long will it take?** Half-an-hour, an afternoon – or would it be best split into two or three short sessions?

• **What preparations do you need to make?** Do you need to practise the skill yourself or ask someone to teach you first – or should you ask someone else to take the training activity for you?

• **What equipment will you need?** Is it available when you want to use it? Do you need to buy anything – food to cook, for example? If so, who will get it and who will pay? What happens to the equipment afterwards – who cleans it and returns it?

• **What is the most exciting and interesting way to present the activity?** Will you need visual aids? Are there books that will help? Can the skill be learned through a game or a project that will hold the Scouts' attention?

•**How can you keep the Scouts' interest?** If you are practising a skill that everyone should know, can you think of a new way or a new slant to try?

## And afterwards . . .

When the training activity is over, here are three questions to ask yourself and to discuss with your Assistant Patrol Leader:

•**What happens next?** The Scouts who took part have learned something new – how can they (and other Scouts) take part in another activity using that skill?

•**Can we take the training a step further?** Are there parts of awards or Proficiency Badges that we can work for now that we have learned a new skill?

•**How did the training activity go?** Was it fun? Did those taking part learn something? Was the instruction good enough? Does the instructor need to brush up on the skill himself or did he talk over the heads of the Scouts?

## Awards and badges

As a Patrol Leader it is up to you to encourage Scouts to pass the requirements of the Scout Award and of the Explorer Award, and to make arrangements for them to do so. They will need training and some of that training you will give, while asking others to help you with this, too.

Your Scout Leader will want your help with the arrangements being made for training and passing the requirements of the Pathfinder Award and the Chief Scout's Award. It is the same with Proficiency Badges and all these things will be discussed at the Patrol Leaders' Council.

The Scouts in your Patrol will look to you for help in making progress and making sure that they have the chance to do so is a very important part of your work as a Patrol Leader.

Above all, be enthusiastic about the training activities you arrange. You may feel your heart sinking into your boots at the thought of having to teach yet another Scout how to tie a bowline, but for that Scout it will be something *new* – and if you show that you want him to learn and are keen and interested, he will be, too. You may be bored by bowlines, but it is the Scout you are teaching who is important and if he enjoys learning, that's all that really matters.

Action 5

# Challenge

Rig up a sisal line between two trees about 3m (10ft) above ground level, and just beyond it set down two billies of water. Mark out a baseline 5m (16ft) from the two billies. Divide the Patrol into two teams. Provide sisal, garden canes, rubber bands, mallets and two small pulley blocks for each team – and challenge them to see which team can lift their billy over the sisal line and onto their baseline first. The teams may not go beyond the baseline.

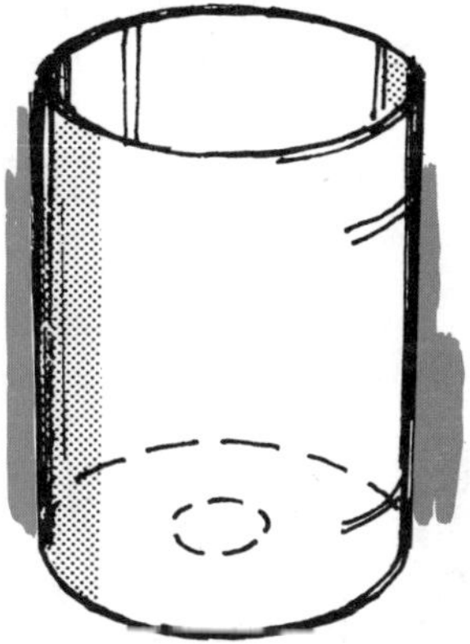

*For this sawdust stove you will need an old five-gallon oil drum or a metal bucket that's no longer required for anything else. Make a 65mm (2½ins) hole in the base.*

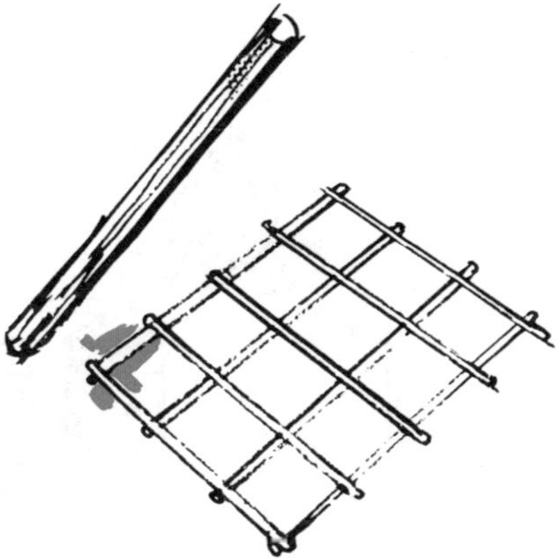

*Make a tapered wooden peg, 75mm (3ins) longer than the depth of the drum. Find an old metal grid for the drum top.*

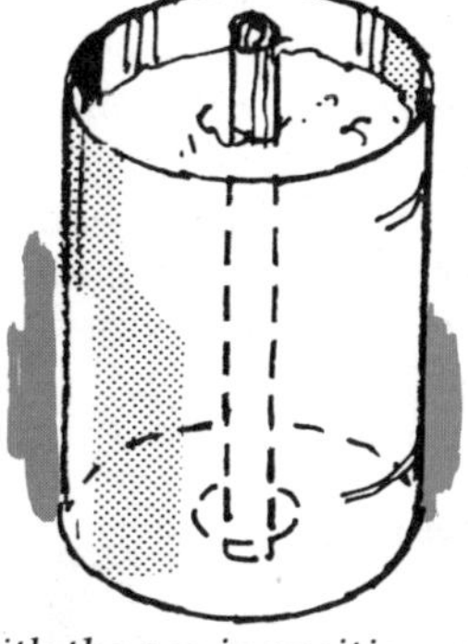

*With the peg in position, pack sawdust tightly into the drum, to within 50mm (2ins) of the top. When the sawdust is well packed and firm, carefully screw the wooden peg out, leaving a hole through the centre.*

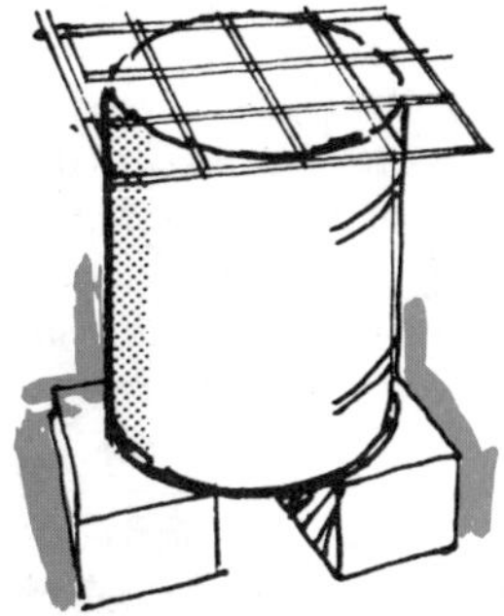

*Stand the drum on bricks outdoors. Light a small fire under the hole in the base of the drum to catch the sawdust alight. One drum of sawdust will burn for three to four hours. Boil, fry or barbecue food on the grid.*

# It's a knockout

Each Patrol brings the equipment and sets up one or two events, and the Patrols try their skills at them all.

*In* Buck-it-up, *the cyclist supports two buckets at either end of a bar across the handlebars of a bicycle. As he cycles down the course, two other Scouts run alongside, throwing the balls into the two buckets. No ball may be used twice. The game ends when the cyclist reaches the finishing line and the winning Patrol is the one with the most balls in the buckets.*

*For* Bumpy-ride, *you need a wheelbarrow and other items as shown. One Scout pushes the wheelbarrow over the bumps whilst another sits inside holding the bucket filled with water. Winners are the Patrol to get the most water into the far bucket in a set time.*

*Called* Bounce, *this requires the first Scout to throw a number of balls onto the first board, where the Scouts holding the board bounce the balls onto the second board. Here the Scouts bounce the balls into the hands of the 'catcher'.*

Cycle-o-rama *finds two Scouts cycling around markers, collecting footballs from a box and attempting to drop them into a bin in the centre. Top score for the Patrol getting the most balls into the bin.*

*Two Patrols compete against each other in* Balloon fishing. *The first Patrol stands inside a roped circle holding broom handles. One member of the opposing Patrol runs round the outside of the circle trailing ten balloons. Each lap covered by the runner scores two points and each balloon not burst counts for another two.*

*Three Scouts stand on a bench, each with a bucket, in* Target tennis. *Another Scout stands in front with a tennis racket and attempts to volley balls thrown by the last Scout on the start line over his head so that the Scouts on the bench catch them in their buckets.*

Sack football *is a good game to end the evening, with Patrols taking part in a knock-out contest. The aim is to score goals as in football – the first goal scored wins the game.*

Offer to run an *It's a knockout* at a District Patrol Leaders' weekend or invite Patrols from another Troop to join your Patrols for an *It's a knockout* evening. These – and similar games that you can devise – are fun in camp; try them at your next father and son or mum and son camp.

# Coracles

A good size for a coracle is about 1.5m (5ft) long, 1m (3ft) wide and 35cm (15ins) deep.

Use sticks about 2cm ($\frac{3}{4}$in) thick for the framework. Choose something that will bend, such as willow, chestnut or ash.

Soak the timber in water for a day before starting work on the frame. Push the sticks into the ground to make an oval outline of the size of coracle you want to build. Bend the tops over and interweave them. Lash down opposite pairs. Three pairs each way will do, but then work in some diagonal ones as well.

See that the central area is fairly flat. Put heavy stones on top and peg the centre down overnight if necessary.

Weave other lighter pieces around the sides. Lash strips around the top of the sides before you pull the main sticks from the ground – these will help to keep the shape you have been trying to achieve. Cut the stakes partly through so that they can be bent down and lashed around the rim.

Stretch a piece of stout polythene sheeting over the framework and lash or nail this to the gunwale (the top of the sides) all round. Fix a plank across the centre as a seat and make sure there are plenty of sticks lashed into position where your feet will come.

Make a paddle from a broom handle with a circular piece of wood fixed at one end. To propel the coracle, sit in the centre and lean forwards while pushing the water back on alternate sides.

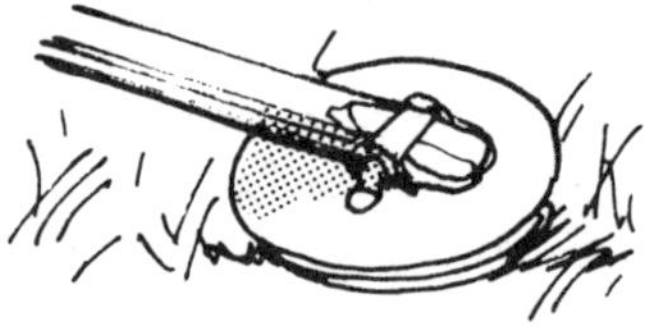

Chapter 7

# Programme planning

Scouts join your Patrol and your Troop for activities – and mainly for activities in the outdoors – but for Scouts, Patrol Leaders or Scouters, finding sufficient time to do all the things you would like to do is often the problem. There are other commitments – at school or work, in the home and the community, at places of worship, in clubs and societies to which we belong. The time that can be given to Scouting is limited, so it is important that the time that is available is well spent. Planning ahead means that limited time can be used to the best advantage.

## Preparation

The Patrol Leaders' Council is the place where programme planning is carried out. Your regular meetings should have an item on the agenda so that you can check how your plans for future programmes are going, but from time to time you will need to have special meetings for programme planning and nothing else.

Whilst the responsibility for programme planning rests with the Scouters and Patrol Leaders, you should involve others. Few people like being told what to do and are much happier if they feel that they have had the opportunity to contribute their ideas in the early stages.

The Patrol-in-Council is where it all starts, with Scouts in the Patrols talking about the things they would like to do – training, activities, camps, expeditions and so on. These ideas are then brought by the Patrol Leaders to the Patrol Leaders' Council.

Other adults who help the Troop – Venture Scouts, Assistant Scout Leaders, parents, Scouters in other Sections – will have ideas, too, but they need to be asked and to feel that their views are wanted.

Here are some points to remember as you get down to programme planning:

- **Keep** other Sections of the Group advised of your plans so that you don't arrange a weekend camp when the tentage is already booked for the Cub Scout Pack or go off on a hike when the Troop should be helping with the summer fête.
- **Inform** the Group Scouters' Meeting and Group Executive Committee of your plans. You may need some special equipment or financial help and the Scout Leader will want to be briefed.
- **Advise** parents of your plans. Many will be interested in what their sons are doing, although it must be admitted that some will not appear to mind one way or the other. If you suddenly announce in early July that summer camp is in four weeks' time and the cost will be £50, don't be surprised if there are problems in getting a 100 per cent turnout. Those parents who want to support you may have arranged their holidays at that time and most will need a little warning before they can find £50 – just like that!
- **Be flexible.** The great thing about having a planned programme over a month or two is that you don't have to stick to it rigidly. If a suggestion or an opportunity comes along and it is something that the Patrol or Troop will enjoy, be

flexible and make room for it in your programme. If you find out that a Troop from overseas will be camping locally in two weeks' time and want to have a joint activity with you, don't turn down the opportunity just because you have planned a hike for that Troop Night. You can hike in your home area at almost any time in the year – but you may not get the chance to meet Scouts from another country for some time.

•**Find** different ways to tackle a familiar subject. A knotting relay race may be fun the first time, but the excitement palls if all your knotting activities consist of relay races.

•**Safety.** There will always be an element of risk in anything we do – even in such familiar things as walking upstairs or crossing the road. Some activities will require the minimum of training: others demand a lot more. Make sure that before an activity is tackled, those involved know the basic skills and are aware of any special safety rules. If you are bridging a stream, you'll want to be sure that the lashings are the right ones for the job and are secure *before* anyone goes across. If canoeing is the activity, an ability to swim and a clear understanding of the safety rules are *essential*. Don't take unnecessary risks – get the training right *first*.

Having the correct equipment for the job is vital, too. Worn ropes or lifejackets that are unsafe are potentially lethal and should not be used.

Take advice from adults who know, follow the Activity Rules in *Policy, Organisation and Rules* and keep risks to an absolute minimum.

## Ideas galore!

Where do ideas for programmes come from? The Scout Section Training Programme (particularly the option lists in the Pathfinder and Chief Scout's Awards and Proficiency Badges), books, magazines, training courses, visits to other Troops, past experience – all these will help.

Try brainstorming. Start with each Patrol having its own brainstorming session, so that the Patrol Leaders can bring ideas from their Patrols to a similar session involving the Scouters and other adults who help with the Troop.

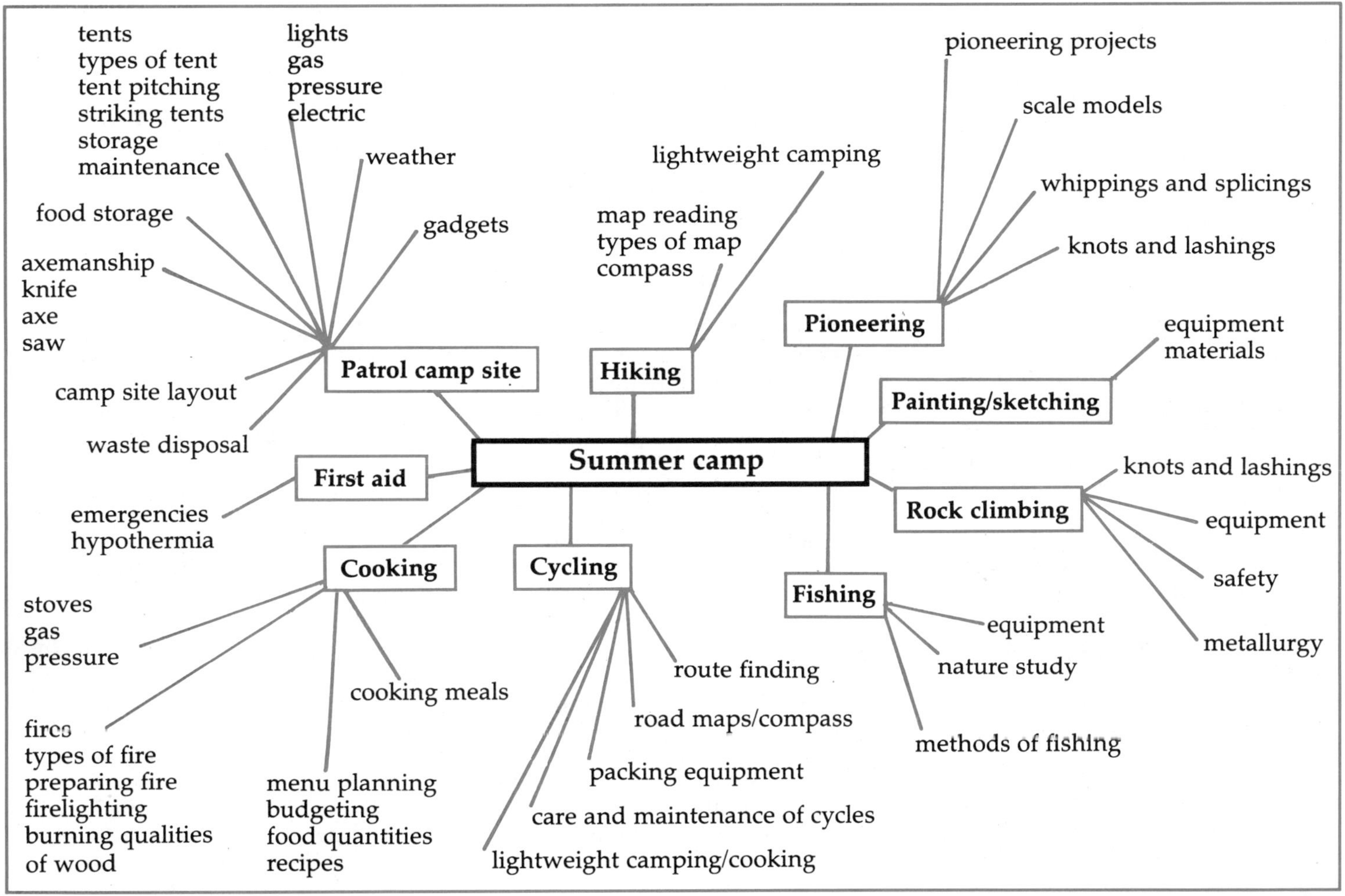
Summer camp
Patrol camp site
tents
types of tent
tent pitching
striking tents
storage
maintenance
lights
gas
pressure
electric
weather
gadgets
food storage
axemanship
knife
axe
saw
camp site layout
waste disposal
Hiking
map reading
types of map
compass
lightweight camping
Pioneering
pioneering projects
scale models
whippings and splicings
knots and lashings
Painting/sketching
equipment
materials
Rock climbing
knots and lashings
equipment
safety
metallurgy
Fishing
equipment
nature study
methods of fishing
Cycling
route finding
road maps/compass
packing equipment
care and maintenance of cycles
lightweight camping/cooking
Cooking
stoves
gas
pressure
fires
types of fire
preparing fire
firelighting
burning qualities
of wood
menu planning
budgeting
food quantities
recipes
cooking meals
First aid
emergencies
hypothermia

Let's assume that your main activity during the next few months will be your annual camp. The Patrol Leaders and Scouters have found a site by a river in good hiking country. Take a large sheet of paper and some felt pens and write 'summer camp' in the centre. Ask those present to think of all the activities they will expect to be involved in at that camp. Some of the activities will be obvious, such as tent pitching, cooking and the like – but write them on the sheet near the centre just the same.

The fact that there is a river may suggest to someone that pioneering might be an activity at summer camp. Hiking could be another – and someone might suggest cycling as well. One or two older Scouts have been doing some rock climbing at school and tell you that their instructor was once a Scout and would be prepared to help with training before and during summer camp if the dates fit in with his own holidays.

When you have listed all the main activities, start to break each one down to show the training that will be necessary if the Scouts are to be prepared to take part in these when the camp arrives. The chart on the previous page shows how the ideas grow from the centre – and build up a list of training subjects that need to be tackled at Patrol and Troop Meetings in the months leading up to the main annual camp. And there are the bones of your programme planning, waiting to be slotted into the week by week meetings of the Patrols and Troop.

A chart like this suggests a number of activities for training sessions, some of which will help your Scouts to make progress in the Scout Section Training Programme, but all of which will prepare everyone for an enjoyable and worthwhile annual camp at the same time.

## Getting started

Don't be put off by the thought of planning your Patrol and Troop programmes ahead. There are no hard and fast rules; you don't have to use complicated charts and you can make it as simple or as complicated as you wish.

For some leaders, programme planning will work using a sheet of paper with the months and weeks down the left hand side and half a dozen columns in which to write the activities, whilst others who enjoy the mechanics of planning may want to put the lot on their home computer. How you set about it is unimportant – and a scheme on a home computer is not necessarily going to be any more (or less) effective than one that's jotted down on a single sheet. What is important is that Scouts enjoy the Scouting they came into your Patrol and Troop for. Planning ahead enables you to check that a wide variety of activities will be offered over the weeks and months so that Scouts make personal progress and have the training that's necessary for camps, expeditions and specialist activities.

The suggestions here are for an overall programme for a year, which is then broken down into seasonal, monthly and weekly programmes. But it is only a suggested scheme – and the Patrol Leaders and Scouters in your Troop need to devise a system that works for them. The system you use is not important: it's the activities that follow that matter.

## Annual programme

Ideally an annual programme needs to start as far away as possible from the main event that you are working towards. If you are planning your main camp for August, then the previous September is a good time to start; if the Spring Bank Holiday is the best time for a main event, then June might be the first month of your Scout Troop's year.

Draw up a year-at-a-glance chart, showing the months down the left hand side with five columns across the page headed (1) theme for the month, (2) Patrol and Troop activities, (3) special events, (4) camps and expeditions and (5) Group, District, County and National events.

If your Scout year starts in September and you are holding your first planning meetings in August, you may know the dates of some events for column (5) – and these can be pencilled in. You may have to wait until January or February for details of events in the spring and summer, but these can be added to the chart when they are known. The advantage of listing events outside the Troop in this way is that you may find that something is being arranged that will fit in with your own plans. For example, one of your training themes might be pioneering and if the District is running a Pioneer Badge course in February, you may decide to make pioneering the theme for that month – and arrange for one or two Scouts from each Patrol to go on the District course to gain wider experience.

Next, look at the results of your brainstorming sessions and list the training topics you want to cover in the months leading up to your main event. If the Patrol Leaders look through their Patrol progress charts showing the achievements of each Scout, they will be able to note the subjects that need to be tackled so that individual Scouts can complete their next award. List the topics and put them side by side with those that came from the brainstorming session.

Now decide on a theme for each month of the year – themes that will include all the training topics that

you have listed (or as many as you can fit in!). Write in the themes on the year-at-a-glance chart – hiking for September, cycling for November, first aid and emergencies for December – and so on. Now complete the other columns – showing how the theme of the month will be developed in Patrol and Troop Meetings, at special events, and in camps and expeditions.

Hiking might suggest map and compass work at Patrol meetings, an orienteering competition on a Troop Night, an afternoon special event at the local camp site trying out some lightweight cooking, plus a day hike for the younger Scouts and a weekend lightweight hike camp for the older members of the Troop – the bare bones of an exciting month's programme.

If you do this in outline for each of the twelve months, you will see an active programme building up – with plenty of time ahead to book camp sites, check equipment, ask people to help with instruction and so on.

## Seasonal programme

For more detailed planning, divide the year into seasons. You may prefer to have three or four seasons – three could be autumn (September to December), spring (January to April) and summer (May to August), whilst four could be autumn (September to November), winter (December to February), spring (March to May) and summer (June to August).

Review each season's plans on the year-at-a-glance chart at least a month before the season begins. You may decide to change a theme for a month because the need for some other training has become obvious or an opportunity to take part in another activity or event that you don't want to miss has come your way.

Make up a seasonal chart with the months and weeks down the left hand side and six columns across the page headed (1) Patrol Leader training, (2) Patrol activities, (3) Troop activites, (4) special events, (5) camps and expeditions, and (6) other events. Write in the theme for each month and be more specific about the activities you will run to develop the training. At this stage write in the names of Patrol Leaders, Scouters and other adults who will take responsibility for organising training and activities – and make sure that they agree to do so.

The column for Patrol Leader training is an important one, for it reminds the Patrol Leaders' Council that they may need to undertake training themselves before they attempt to pass on knowledge or to lead activities during the next few

weeks – and time can be allocated to this.

When the season's programme is planned, let the Group Scouters' Meeting have a copy and inform the Scouts and their parents of dates of afternoon or day activities, weekend camps and so on.

## Monthly programme

Have a monthly programme chart showing the date, the activity and who will run it, as well as any special equipment that may be needed and where the activity will be held. Draw this up for one of your regular Patrol Leaders' Council meetings so that it can be checked through about two or three weeks before the month actually begins. Most of the information will come from your seasonal planning chart, but here you are making final decisions on dates and activities – whilst still being flexible enough to change things if necessary.

## Weekly programme

A short session at the end of Troop Meeting or on another night during the week for Patrol Leaders and Scouters will be the time to check through next week's programme to make sure that everything is prepared and ready.

This short period when the Patrol Leaders and Scouters get together could be used for any final training the Patrol Leaders may need for their part in the activities, for deciding who will run the games, who will instruct, if adults manning bases or running activities have been briefed and will be available – all the last minute things to ensure that the programmes you have planned get off the ground.

## Planning for . . .

The aim of planning is to ensure that Patrol and Troop programmes are fun and worthwhile, and that all Scouts have regular opportunity to make real progress in their awards.

If you achieve this with a computer printout *or* with large sheets of paper pinned to the walls and felt pens *or* in a cheap notebook from the nearest chainstore – that's fine. What matters is *not* the way you plan your programmes, but that your Scouts go home from Troop Night or a Patrol meeting having enjoyed what they have done and just bursting to come again next week and the week after that.

The goal of every Patrol Leader and Scout Leader should be to ensure that everyone moves a little bit forward in the Scout Training Programme by the end of each meeting or activity.

# Troop Night

The weekly meeting is important, for it is through this that a Scout enjoys the companionship of others in his Patrol and joins in activities with Scouts in all the other Patrols.

It is desirable that most weekly meetings start and finish at a set time and place, and have a familiar format. However, that does not mean that the Troop has to fall into a routine that is unchanged and unchangeable. If occasionally the meeting place is different and the format is altered, the element of surprise will help to retain interest.

In these *Action* pages we look at different types of programme for the weekly meeting.

## Troop Night – that's different

The traditional Troop Meeting has a firm place in the programme, with games, Patrol competitions and instruction sessions followed by activities in which the new skills are tried out, but once a month or so a change in the style of programme will be welcome. We look first at traditional Troop Meetings – and then at four ways in which this pattern might be varied.

## Troop Meetings

Here are two programmes in outline. . .

**Programme 1**

*Theme*: stoves and cooking.

*On arrival*: each Scout is given a knotting rope. The Patrols produce one continuous rope with a different knot at each join. Using the rope, Patrols devise a gadget useful in camp and demonstrate it.

*Flag break/inspection (10 mins.)*: by Scout Leader.

*Game (10 mins.)*: run by Assistant Scout Leader.

*Training (15 mins.)*: Patrol Leaders instruct their Patrols on lighting and maintaining pressure stoves.

*Game (10 mins.)*: run by a Patrol Leader.

*Activity – observation (10 mins.)*: Assistant Scout Leader has collected a dozen different sweaters/T-shirts often worn by members of the Scout Group. Each is numbered and hung on a line stretched across the hall. Patrols examine them – and make a list of their owners.

*Training activity – cooking (30 mins.)*: using pressure stoves, Patrols cook a simple meal for the Patrol Leader of another Patrol (eggs and bacon, followed by pancakes and a cup of tea). To keep everyone involved, hand Patrols a duplicated sheet with a cooking quiz for them to complete.

*Just for fun (10 mins.)*: find the Scout who can stand on one leg for the longest time or the Patrol that can keep silent longest.

*Notices, ceremonies, flag down, prayers (5 mins.)*

**Programme 2**
*Theme:* basic skills
*On arrival:* as each Scout arrives he looks at a tray of 20 objects for a minute – and then joins his Patrol where they make up a list together.
*Flag break/inspection (10 mins.):* an Assistant Scout Leader inspects, while the Scout Leader checks each Patrol's list.
*Game (10 mins.):* run by a Patrol Leader.
*Training activity (25 mins.):* set up a trading post with three tables, each manned by an adult leader or helper. Table 1 sells raw materials (tea, milk, sugar, rope ends, whipping twine, strips of leather, pencils, paper etc.). Table 2 sells tools and appliances for hire. Charge 5p for ten minutes and have things like stoves, cooking utensils, mugs, spoons, mixing bowls etc. Table 3 is the sales counter where the finished articles are sold by the Patrols. Give each Patrol 100p to start – slips of card with values written on them – plus a list of things they are to make and the selling price of each (generally 10p per item). Suggestions for things to make are: a hot drink, a sailmaker's whipping, a plaster cast, a tent peg, backsplice and eyesplice, six knots in one length of rope, a drawing of 12 road signs (making sure you have the raw materials and the tools and appliances for whatever is on your list).
*Game (10 mins.):* break off for a game run by an Assistant Scout Leader.
*Training activity (20 mins.):* complete trading post.
*Just for fun (10 mins.):* hang a sheet of paper on the wall listing 20 items each Patrol is to find around your Headquarters. Just to be different, hang the sheet of paper upside down and ask the Patrols to display their items upside down, too.
*Notices, ceremonies, flag down, prayers (5 mins.)*

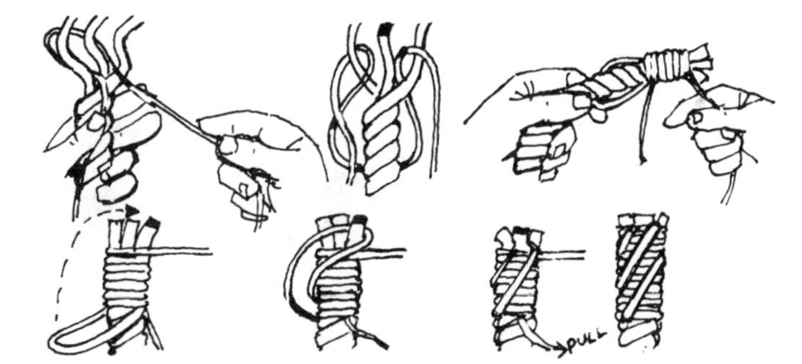

*Sailmaker's whipping – unlay the end of the rope about 5cm (2in) and start with a loop of whipping twine around one strand. End with a reef knot on the crown.*

## Patrol project night

As a variation on the Troop Meeting format, the Patrols spend the evening of the weekly meeting on a project. The Patrols meet under their own arrangements for the project, but come together as a Troop at the end of the evening for a game and any ceremonies.

Projects might be:

**Local knowledge quiz:** have two sets of questions for each Patrol – one for the younger Scouts and another for the older Scouts, or one for those on foot and another for those on cycles.
**Scavenge hunt:** list the objects the Patrols are to bring back or observe.
**Cooking:** a Patrol barbecue in someone's garden or on the local camp site, with each Patrol inviting an adult leader as their guest.
**Patrol newspaper:** give each Patrol some large

sheets of paper, felt pens, pictorial magazines, scissors – and they make their own newspaper of local happenings that evening.

**Camp planning:** Patrols prepare menu, food list, gear list, site layout, programme and details of transport arrangements for their next Patrol camp.

**Pioneering:** Patrols build a ballista using garden canes and rubber bands, practise with it – and use it in an inter-Patrol activity when the Troop meets at the end of the evening.

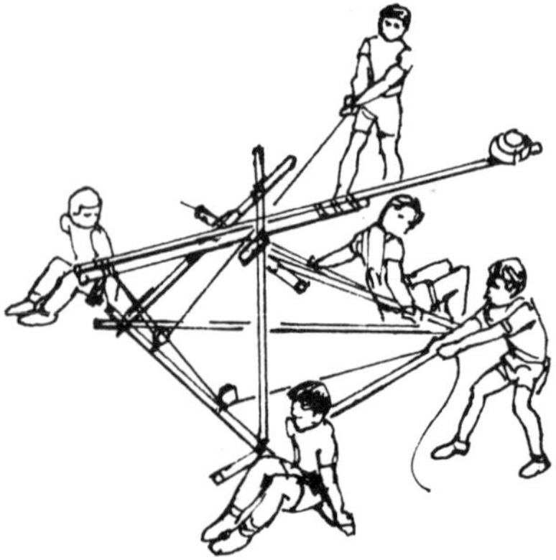

## Circuit activities

Start and close the Troop Meeting in the usual way, and have a lively game at the beginning, one halfway through and another at the end of the evening.

For the rest of the time the Scouts move around a series of bases, where they try out a new skill, revise something through an activity or receive instruction. The bases are manned by Patrol Leaders, adult leaders, parents – anyone with a skill to offer can be asked to help. The Troop could work in Patrols, spending 15 minutes at each base, or the Scouts could be divided into groups by age or interest and spending, say, 30 minutes at each of two bases during the evening.

Check which skills in the Progressive Awards need to be tackled, brief those who are looking after each base and make sure that the equipment needed is available. Try to use any spare rooms or places around your meeting hall, so that the Patrols do not get in each other's way and to give those instructing a chance to concentrate on what they are doing.

*Creative activity – find a parent or adult leader whose hobby might interest Scouts in trying something new for themselves.*

**Circuit activities 1** (for Patrols)
*Theme:* Pioneering
*Base A:* Turk's head woggles (in hall).
*Base B:* Highwayman's hitch descending from tree (outside).
*Base C:* Practise whipping rope ends (Group store).
*Base D:* Pioneering models (nearby house).

**Circuit activities 2** (in groups of Scouts – those under 13 taking part in A and B – and those over 13 or who have completed these parts of the Progressive Awards tackle C and D).
*Theme:* New skills
*Base A:* Tent pitching (outside).
*Base B:* Map and compass navigation exercise (outside).
*Base C:* Creative activity (in home of an adult who demonstrates his hobby).
*Base D:* Emergency procedures (with Venture Scouts as instructors in hall).

## Patrol instruction night

Each Patrol (or age or interest group) tackles a different activity for a complete Troop Night. If you have four Patrols (or decide to make up six special interest groups) you will need that number of activities. Ask Patrol Leaders, adult leaders, parents or outside experts to lead each activity.

Once you have decided on the number of groups, you could arrange to run this programme on, say, the first Troop Night every month – until all the groups have tackled each activity. Instructors from outside may be prepared to help one evening a month, but might find it difficult to commit themselves to an evening four (or more) weeks running.

Here is a selection of activities (and there are plenty more in the Award Training Scheme):

**Swimming:** visit the nearest pool with an instructor to assess training needs for individual Scouts – and plan this over the next few weeks.

**Knotting:** an evening with an expert – moving from knots and lashings to making woggles, lanyards, decorative knots etc.

**Cooking:** in the kitchen at the Scout Headquarters or in the instructor's home.

**Emergencies:** visit an ambulance, police or fire station.

**Backwoods cooking:** at the local camp site.

**Survey:** examine traffic conditions or local industry.

**Carpentry:** Patrols work with someone whose hobby is carpentry in making items of equipment for camp (fold-up chairs, a hay box or slatted roll-up table top, for example).

**Sport:** take part in a sport at your nearest sports centre.

**Equipment maintenance:** Patrols work with the Group Quartermaster, preparing for camp.

**Photography:** working with an enthusiast, the Patrol takes a roll of film and then develops and prints it.

*Cooking – divide the Patrol into two, one group cooking indoors (on gas or electricity) and the other outdoors.*

## Activity night

One big, well-organised and exciting activity night every so often can be a Troop highlight. Take time over the planning. Why not invite a Patrol from another Troop to join you?

Some ideas are:

**Competitive rally:** a series of activities for the Patrols to try in turn over a timed course, such as tent pitching, plaster casting, rope ladder making (and testing), lifeline throwing, sweet making, firelighting and water boiling, making a compass, following a blind trail.

**Treasure hunt:** with a series of clues, each leading to the next. Some clues written on card and hidden, others placed in shop windows (with the co-operation of the local shopkeepers), and others obtained by making a telephone call. Or all the clues could be photographs of parts of local buildings where the next clues are hidden.

**Pancake night:** hold near Shrove Tuesday. Patrols could make pancakes over pressure stoves. Hold a pancake race around your meeting place, followed by a competition for the best served pancake, the most-highly-coloured pancake (using food colourings) and the largest pancake.

**Troop Olympics:** run as an inter-Patrol sports activity with javelin throwing (using garden canes), tent peg relay (knocking a 23cm (9ins) tent peg 15cm (6ins) into the ground), hop, skip and jump, sedan chair race (using two broomsticks to support passenger), discus throwing (using cardboard plates), putting the shot backwards (throwing a plastic football over the head), throwing the hammer (with a wooden mallet) . . . and you will think of other equally crazy ideas. (Make sure that no one gets in the way of any of the flying objects!)

# Programme themes

In Chapter 7 we showed how themes are developed for the monthly programme. Here are some examples of activity themes from the Scout Progressive Award Training Programme, with suggestions for using these at meetings during the month. When planning a month's programme, include time for training sessions for Scouters and Patrol Leaders, so that there is adequate preparation for those meetings which Patrol Leaders will run on their own or where they are required to instruct in a skill.

Sometimes it is necessary to include training for younger Scouts, which would mean that older Scouts find themselves going over familiar ground yet again. Arrange some alternative training for older Scouts (with Venture Scouts, for example) whilst younger members of the Patrols are learning basic skills, but ensure that the activity in which the skills are going to be used will be a test for the younger Scouts and a new challenge for the older ones.

In the outline programmes that follow we have omitted details of games and other parts of the weekly meetings for the sake of brevity.

## Theme: local knowledge

**Week 1: Patrol project night**

Patrols meet under their own arrangements for a scavenge hunt – with a list of things to find and observe locally. Patrols meet as a Troop at the end of the evening to finish.

**Week 2: Circuit activities**

*Base 1:* estimating height.

*Base 2:* estimating width.

*Base 3:* emergency calls from public/home telephone.

*Base 4:* traffic survey at busy junction.

**Week 3: Troop Meeting**

*Patrol activity* – a number of adults are in the area requiring help. Patrols go out to find them. Brief parents and helpers who act as strangers to the area (a visitor from overseas who only speaks French is trying to understand a bus timetable, a woman on a bicycle is studying a road map and wants directions, a man rushes from a house just as a Patrol passes by for help with a burst pipe etc.).

*Patrol activity* – within a time limit, Patrols have to estimate height/width of a number of features outdoors.

**Week 4: Activity night**

A 'know your town' game for an evening or half-day. Give each Patrol an outline street plan, with the names of roads and so on blocked out. List all the things you want Patrols to mark on their outline map – some of which they can find by visiting various locations and others which will require more research (for example, ask the Patrols to mark all the post offices and pillar boxes on the map – and then to find out the 'walks' used by each postman in the town to deliver the post).

## Theme: cooking

**Week 1: Circuit activities**
Patrols tackle two of the four bases (30 mins. at each).
*Base 1:* egg cooking (three stoves – Scouts fry eggs, make scrambled eggs and omelettes).
*Base 2:* sweet making.
*Base 3:* drinks (tea, lemon tea, coffee, cocoa, soups – try different types and experiment with methods of preparation).
*Base 4:* pancakes (mix and cook pancakes – then try apple or banana fritters).

**Week 2: Patrol meeting**
Working in pairs, younger Scouts try their hand at menu planning and preparing food quantity lists, and then make some sweets, whilst older Scouts construct a haybox for the next Patrol camp.

**Week 3: Circuit activities**
Patrols tackle the two bases they missed at the circuit activities meeting in Week 1.

**Week 4: Patrol project night**
Each Patrol arranges its own barbecue (in a garden, at the local camp site, outside your Headquarters), inviting a guest.

**Week 5: Troop Meeting (younger Scouts) and activity night (older Scouts)**
The younger Scouts enjoy a games evening, with some activities from the awards, whilst the older Scouts divide into pairs and cook a backwoods meal at the local camp site.

# Themes and activities

Here are a number of themes based on the Scout Progressive Award Training Programme, with brief details of activities that can be adapted for use at Troop and Patrol meetings, as bases on circuit activity and Patrol instruction nights, for Patrol project nights and activity nights.

## Cycling

- Stripping down, maintaining and repairing, and reassembling a bicycle with an expert.
- *Highway Code*/road safety games, competitions and films.
- National system of road numbering – complete an outline map.
- Cycle sports – slow cycling; walk, run and ride race; relay races; tent peg slalom race.
- Scavenge hunt on cycles.
- Cycle orienteering.
- Cyclo-cross (Patrol could take part in a local club's activities for an evening).
- Cycle camping (with training on selecting equipment, packing and carrying on cycle).

## Map and compass

- Making a compass and finding North without one.
- Relief models from contours on maps.
- Taking an imaginary hike on a map indoors – and then following the route outdoors later (comparing notes of what you expected to find with what's on the ground).
- Plane table mapping.
- Aerial photographs – comparing them to maps (indoors) and on the ground (outdoors).
- Evening or afternoon hike – Patrols start from different places and meet up at central point after following instructions that require map reading skill.

*Visit camping showrooms to compare the prices of new tents.*

## Camping

•Tent survey – assemble a number of different types of tent (borrow from parents and other Scout Groups, too). Patrols prepare a report on advantages and disadvantages of each tent.

•Tent design – Patrols design a new tent – and make it using garden canes, rubber bands and sheets of polythene.

•Modelling – make a model of your camp site for the next Patrol camp.

•Make equipment for camp – collapsible slatted roll-up table tops, ovens, camp larders, storage boxes, axe sheaths, hot water system for fire.

•Experiment with different methods of starting a fire – natural materials (birch bark), waxed newspaper, wire wool and sisal.

•Circuit activity bases: timed firelighting (burning through a piece of string suspended above the fire), erect a flag staff (from garden canes, rubber bands, sisal, tent pegs and mallet), bed-making with blankets and pins, tent packing, turfing, washing-up, lighting and filling a hurricane lamp, sharpening a knife.

## Hikes and expeditions

•Concentrated foods – practise cooking and making up survival packs of these foods.

•Experiment with different types of pressure and gas stoves (borrow additional varieties from parents and other Scout Groups or Venture Scout Units), testing their speed, cooking efficiency and running costs.

•Working from maps, prepare route cards – and then try these out on the ground.

•Practise pitching hike tents – in daylight, in the dark, in total silence (with a tape recorder inside the tent to check afterwards), in bad weather – so that Scouts are prepared for the worst.

•Pack and unpack a rucsac in total darkness.

•Make items of equipment such as map cases.

## Ropework

•Teach (or revise) a knot a week and follow with an activity: prussic knot (hang climbing rope from a beam, Scouts tie loops with prussic knot for footholds and turn it into a rope ladder); barrel hitch (give each Patrol an oil drum or bucket, rope and some bricks – they have to lift the bricks 3m (9ft) off the ground); scaffold hitch (Patrols make a swing, using a scaffold hitch to sling the seat); timber hitch (have a log-hauling race over rough ground).

•Stop-watch knotting: devise a series of challenges using three or four knots (for example, stand two chairs 1m (3ft) apart, take two ropes and tie a clove hitch round the leg of one chair and a round turn and two half hitches round a leg of the other; join both ropes with a sheetbend and then shorten the rope with a sheepshank). Time each Scout in the Patrol, find who does this in the fastest time – and the champions from all the Patrols compete against each other.

- Knotting boards: use two different colours of picture-hanging cord (to show the two ends of the rope used in the knots and lashings) and make as many knots and lashings as you can – pinning them all to a board for your Patrol corner (but only keep it for a month or two as knot boards are great dust-gatherers . . . and, in any case, someone else might like to try their hand at making a better one).
- Whipping and splicing – ask the Group Quartermaster to let the Troop have any new (or worn) ropes that require whipping or splicing. Keep these in a box and encourage every Scout to do a whipping or splicing when he arrives on Troop Night and while he is waiting for starting time.

## Sports

- Ask a keep-fit enthusiast to meet each Patrol in turn and to help each Scout to devise his own personal keep fit programme. Follow up a month or two later to see how things have progressed.
- Arrange for the Patrols to take turns in spending an evening at your nearest sports centre – to watch the various sports and to take part in one.
- Patrols visit a roller skating or ice skating rink, or a ten pin bowling centre (or whatever else is available in your area).
- Apart from visits to a public swimming pool, try to arrange a session where two Patrols will have the pool to themselves (look around for a suitable pool – on the nearest camp site, in a private garden or club). An inter-Patrol competition could include retrieving objects (coins, bricks wrapped in a towel) from the bottom of the pool; dressing race (using an old shirt and shorts); bobbing for apples etc.
- Invite a well-known local sportsman (footballer, cricketer, marathon runner, swimmer, tennis player etc.) to meet a Patrol to teach them the basic skills. Arrange for the Patrol to watch the sportsman at an event or game where he is taking part – and meet him afterwards to discuss his performance.

## Axemanship

- Topics for bases at a circuit activities night – fitting a new haft to a hand-axe; sharpening, oiling and greasing a hand-axe; changing the blades on a saw; masking, carrying and storage of axes and saws in camp; using wedges and a sledgehammer to split logs; using a hand-axe; using a saw.
- Activities for Patrol meetings – maintenance and sharpening sheath knives and penknives; practise preparing wood for a fire; whittling objects in wood (tent pegs, coats of arms, shields, models); making masks and sheaths.

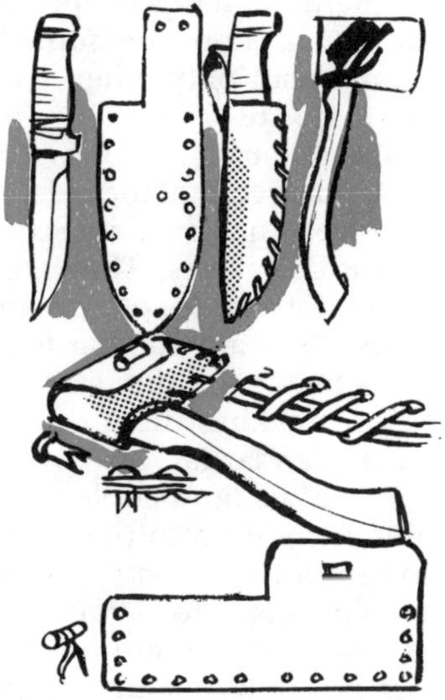

*Make masks for axes and saws at Patrol meetings*

Chapter 8

# Promise and Law

The Scout Promise and the Scout Law are a vital part of everything we do and are not a separate activity. We may have singled them out for mention in this chapter, but they are not options or something we think about only when we remember to do so.

The Promise and Law offer a set of positive standards to be achieved, not only in Scouting but in our daily lives. They are positive – and not a series of do's and don'ts – and they are standards that each of us needs to think carefully about before making them our own personal standards.

In public life people expect to be able to look up to their leaders and to see in them something that they would wish to attain for themselves. Here we are not talking about position and power, but those characteristics of courtesy, of care and concern, of sharing and sympathy, of moral standards, and of appreciating the other person's point of view (while not necessarily having to agree with it).

Occasionally people in public life are shown not to be all that they would have us believe. We respected and admired them, and we feel let down when they are quite the reverse of what we had imagined them to be.

In the same way the Scouts in our Patrols and Troop look to their leaders for example. Scouts expect their leaders to have standards based on the Promise and Law – and will feel let down if they find otherwise. It may not always be obvious, but Scouts will watch and note your reactions – and form their own judgements on you both as a leader and as a person. It is a heavy responsibility that a leader carries in setting the kind of example that a Scout will want to follow for himself. Your standards will be the yardstick by which he measures the attitudes of others but – even more important – they will be the start of his own personal standards.

## The Scout Promise

Our understanding of the Scout Promise and our acceptance of what it entails is a very personal thing, but in addition it affects every aspect of our work as leaders. For this reason it is worth pausing from time to time at a Patrol Leaders' Council to discuss the Promise – what it means to us as individuals

and whether or not the activities we are arranging and the decisions we are making are firmly based on the Promise. Just as we expect a Scout to improve his performance of a skill such as first aid or canoeing, a discussion like this reminds us that the programme we are planning should provide our Scouts and ourselves with the opportunity to grow in understanding and acceptance of the Scout Promise.

The greatest gifts, and the greatest responsibilities, that God has given us are our own lives. And there is the beginning of our Scout Promise: to use God's gift well; to be people who are 'fully alive' as God wants us to be.

A Scout who is 'fully alive' will not just follow the crowd; he will make up his own mind and be ready to accept responsibility for what he does. He will want to develop the abilities God has given him. He will want to be honest with himself and with others.

A Scout who is 'fully alive' will know that other people need his help and that he needs the help of other people. He will be pleased to share with others, to care for others, to work with others. He will be pleased to be with his Patrol.

A Scout who is 'fully alive' will be concerned about the world around us – both town and countryside. The world is God's creation and God has given it into our care. A Scout will want to find out all he can about it. Taking care of where lives; following the *Country Code*; these are just two ways of being concerned about the world about us.

A Scout who is 'fully alive' will have respect for other people. Their lives are as important as his own. He will show that respect in the way he treats others. As far as he can, he will show a special concern for those in need.

A Scout who is 'fully alive' will live as the friend of God. He will speak with Him: to praise Him, to thank Him, to ask for His help. He will listen to God.

The different religions in the world are different ways in which people try to understand and fulfil better their 'duty to God', to be 'fully alive' as God wants us to be. It is certainly part of a Scout's 'duty to God' to try to be as faithful as possible to his own religious faith. It may well be that he is not an active member of any religion. He will then want to find out all that he can so that he may understand better how to be 'fully alive'.

Some questions to spark off a discussion are suggested here:

**On my honour, I promise**

- This is a personal commitment,

but have we as a Patrol Leaders' Council kept our Scout Promise?

- What does honour mean – to us as leaders and to our Scouts?
- Have we let our Scouts down?
- Are we too concerned with imposing our standards rather than helping others to achieve their own?

**that I will do my best**

- This indicates acceptance of the responsibility to be practical and active, and not passive or submissive. Have we shown leadership that gets things done – or have we given in or given up?
- Scouting is about doing – and learning as a result. Have we provided opportunities for ourselves – and for others in the Troop – to learn from their mistakes?
- Do we expect people to do *their* best (and measure their achievements by the progress they have made and the improvements in performance they have shown) or do we set the same standards for all?

**to do my duty to God**

- Are we encouraging everyone – Scouts, Patrol Leaders, Scouters – to grow in their religious faith?
- Do the programmes we arrange widen the opportunities for our members to experience all aspects of their faith?
- Do our activities help our members to meet their religious obligations – or do they put obstacles in their way?
- Do we plan the games, activities, hikes and camps – and leave prayers and religious observances as an afterthought?
- Does our duty to God stop at religious observances or does it take us out into the wider community?
- When did we last discuss moral issues in the context of our faith – or is this something we always put off for another time? Is there someone we can ask to help us to develop this?
- Do we involve our ministers of religion and chaplains in planning and carrying out activities that will enable our Scouts to grow in their faith?
- Do we know the religious faith of all our members and are we actively interested in helping them to carry out that faith in practice?

**and to the Queen**

- Are the standards of conduct accepted by the society in which we live the same standards that we expect from ourselves and from the Scouts in our Patrols and Troop – or do we expect more or try to get away with something less?
- Do we turn a blind eye when we should be making a stand? How concerned are we about dishonesty, for example? If all the Troop's duplicating paper is taken from a place of work and brought home without the permission of the employer, do we accept that this is theft – or do we kid ourselves otherwise?
- Does our training programme help our members to understand how the community – both locally and nationally – runs its affairs, and to appreciate that they have an increasing part to play?

**to help other people**

- Does the Patrol Leaders' Council look for ways in which members can be of service to others – individually, as Patrols or as a Troop?
- Is 'service' a one-off good turn each year – and then nothing until next Christmas?
- Longer-term commitments (to an elderly person, for example) can be helpful, but is the Patrol Leaders' Council certain that it can fulfil what is required week by week – or

will you be letting someone down when the enthusiasm wears off?
•Is helping others a 'project' or something that should be happening all the time?
•Is helpfulness a characteristic we expect amongst our members?

**and to keep the Scout Law**

•Taking each of the seven Scout Laws in turn, does the Patrol Leaders' Council consider that each one is reflected in the life and attitudes of the Patrols and Troop – and of the Patrol Leaders' Council, too?
•Is there a feeling of trust amongst members?
•Is there a sense of loyalty amongst members – to each other, to their Patrols, to the Troop and to Scouting? Does loyalty stop there?
•Are people friendly? Are Cub Scouts and new members made to feel welcome?
•Does brotherhood mean anything – or are there groups within the Troop who will have little to do with anyone else (and is there a danger that the Patrol Leaders' Council is going that way)?
•Is courage only a matter of muscle and is that the only kind of courage that finds reward? Are you aware of

members who are showing a different sort of courage in overcoming what to others may appear to be minor disabilities, but which require just as much determination from the Scouts involved?
•Is a Scout's personal respect for himself ever discussed: have you ever discussed this – honestly – as a Patrol Leaders' Council?
•Is time wasted?
•Is equipment treated with care – or does it come too easily?
•Do Scouts respect the views, feelings, opinions and attitudes of others – in their Patrol, at home, at school and in the wider community? How might the activities of the Troop help in this?

Since Scouting is available to those who follow all religions, it must take account of different religious obligations. Similarly, Scouts from other countries may owe an allegiance to their own Head of State. To meet these circumstances, there are different forms of the Scout Promise that can be made, allowing for the individual's obligations and upholding the spirit of the Promise. A variation is known as the Outlander Promise.

Duty to God implies the acceptance of Divine Guidance and according to the actual religion, the word 'God' would be replaced by 'Allah', 'My Dharma', 'My religion' or others as appropriate. Duty to the Queen would be replaced by 'the country in which I am now living', but it should be noted that British Subjects must accept duty to the Queen.

The decision as to which formula should be adopted is made by the Group Scout Leader in consultation with the District Commissioner. The Association's Headquarters at Baden-Powell House would be pleased to advise on these matters. It is important to recognise a Scout's nationality status, to be fully aware of the exact nature of his religion and to ensure that the Promise taken is as fully binding to him personally as that taken by all other members.

# Standards

The Patrol Leaders' Council is responsible for setting standards and for seeing that those standards are discussed, understood and maintained.

There are physical standards (of safety, camping, hygiene and uniform), mental standards (recognising that each member will start from a different baseline and that you will be looking for personal improvement) and spiritual standards (involving growth in understanding and awareness, and an ability to put faith into practice).

Matters of discipline are the concern of the Patrol Leaders' Council and in this personal example counts, for those who would set out to help others must expect to find their own actions subjected to a similar critical analysis.

If there is a lack of discipline in the Patrol or Troop, chaos follows shortly behind. It may be fun at the start, but Scouts will soon become fed up if everyone plays about and little is achieved. Sometimes problems will be caused by one or two individuals and the Patrol Leaders' Council has to be ready to take an unpopular course of action. This may upset some, but if it will benefit the majority, it has to be carried through.

The Patrol Leaders' Council should discuss ways of encouraging Scouts to accept personal responsibility for their actions as well as a team spirit within the Patrols and the Troop. Sometimes a points system or inter-Patrol challenges will be helpful – and at other times they can have the opposite effect. It's fine if your Patrol is winning all the points – but it can be very depressing if you are trailing behind.

In life we have to accept both success and failure, but when a points system becomes a one-sided affair, we need to find a way for those who are not doing too well to prove their ability in other things. A points system at summer camp is great if our Patrol is in front, but if after a few days it becomes clear to the Patrol that is trailing last that there is no way in which they can catch up, rather than encourage high standards, it may have the reverse effect. One way to overcome this is to introduce an activity or a competition that is separate from the points system and one that will give the Patrol that is trailing behind an equal chance of achieving success. For example, the Patrol Leaders' Council could introduce a Camping Standard which every Patrol has the chance to reach. Successful Patrols could display a decorated tent peg or pennant.

Standards of achievement in the training programme are the responsibility of the Patrol Leaders' Council, with personal goals being set for each member so that he attains his best.

When the Patrol Leaders' Council discusses matters of discipline, behaviour and achievement, difficult decisions will often have to be made. Be fair and give everyone the opportunity to put his point of view across. Don't be afraid to ask advice before reaching your decision. Listen to what others have to say and don't judge the issue before you have heard all the facts.

When a decision is made and a course of action decided upon, it should be supported by every member of the Patrol Leaders' Council. One or two members may disagree, but a collective decision of the Patrol Leaders' Council should have the backing of everyone once it has been made.

## Leadership

It is said that too often adults give their children bunches of cut flowers when they should be helping them to grow their own plants. As Patrol Leaders and Scouters it is often easier – and less trouble – to do everything yourself and to provide activities already planned in every detail, but leadership is about encouraging others to achieve things for themselves.

Few leaders are born – most are made. Scouting provides a unique chance for leaders to be made – if members are allowed to take initiatives, with Patrol Leaders and adults on hand to offer help beforehand and encouragement afterwards, but not interference whilst the activity is taking place (unless a matter of safety is involved – and only then).

As leaders you have responsibilities to yourself and to others (to Scouts, to their parents and to the community). As a leader you are there to:

**Get things done.** Plan first, involve others, involve yourself, but be ready to stand back so that you can see what's happening. If you are setting up camp, give everyone something to do and take on a job for yourself that is just as demanding as the others, but which enables you to keep an eye on things. Don't stand back and supervise – and expect everyone else to do the hard work. Use people's skills, but encourage them to accept the challenge of learning something new.

**Keep the group together.** Make sure that everyone feels involved and has a contribution to make to the task in hand. Encourage and persuade, rather than issue orders. See that everyone is happy in what they are doing and help them to work together.

**Accept responsibility for each individual in the group.** People like to be wanted and to feel that their part in the task is important. People are different and some may need more attention, help or encouragement than others. Avoid favouritism. Praise a person's good points and do not just look for faults. Explain why you are tackling a job in a particular way and involve others in the decisions so that they feel part of things.

## Responsibility

Discuss the responsibility of leadership at the Patrol Leaders' Council. Later you might invite others who provide leadership in their lives to join you for discussion – parents, teachers, people at work and those at your place of worship.

Leaders have responsibilities to:

- themselves;
- their Patrols – if they are Patrol Leaders;
- their Troop – if they are Patrol Leaders or Scout Leaders;
- their Scout Group;
- Scouting in general.

But there are wider responsibilities to:

- family;
- friends;
- work or school;
- the religious community to which you belong;
- the community at large.

# Promise and Law activities

**Meal**

Invite a leader at your place of worship to a meal which the Patrol has cooked. The meal could be in the home of a member of the Patrol (if the Scout's parents have sufficient trust in the way you will do things, they may be prepared to go out for an hour or so – in that way the meal will be very much the Patrol's own). You may prefer to cook the meal outdoors – at the local camp site or in someone's garden.

Talk with your guest to find out when he can come and where the meal will be. Make sure that everyone in the Patrol helps in some way. Parents may be willing to help with supplying some of the food to keep the cost down.

*Make sure that you welcome your guest to the meal the Patrol has cooked and that the table is properly set.*

**Act of worship**

Discuss at a Patrol-in-Council meeting how the Patrol might arrange a short act of worship, either at the end of a Troop Meeting or in camp.

You might invite a leader from your place of worship to come to a later meeting to help you choose some readings, hymns or songs, and to suggest the form the prayers might take.

Some members of the Patrol could lead the readings or prayers – and others might help by playing a musical instrument or by making things to use at the act of worship. Talk about this – someone might make a symbol of your religion, another a stand for the holy book to rest on. In this way you can involve all members of the Patrol – some who like reading or making music and others who are good at making things with their hands.

**Influence**

A week or so before your next Patrol meeting, ask each Scout to come prepared to talk to the rest of the Patrol about a person who has influenced their life. It might be their parents, a leader at their place of worship or someone nationally well-known and famous. Ask them to think of someone who has good points that they would like to follow. Don't expect your Scouts to want to talk too long – but encourage them all you can.

**Worship**
Go to your local place of worship with other members of your Patrol who are of the same faith. Find out when there is a service that you believe will have meaning for them if they are not regular attenders. Talk with others at your place of worship and make sure that the Scouts feel welcome and can follow what is going on. Invite them home for coffee afterwards.

**My neighbour**
At a Patrol-in-Council meeting suggest that the Scouts in the Patrol divide into pairs – and go to each other's home to offer to do a job of service for their parents.

Ask around to find out if there are neighbours who could do with some help from time to time – and encourage Scouts to visit them to do odd jobs.

Talk with the leaders at your place of worship – do they know of people who need help occasionally?

**Service to others**
Look around for an organisation in your neighbourhood that offers a service to others – the Samaritans, meals-on-wheels, elderly persons' club, child welfare etc. Ask if someone will speak to the Patrol about their work and then arrange to visit and see things in action for yourselves. Is there some way in which you might help – during the school holidays, perhaps?

**Prayer**
End each Patrol meeting with a short prayer – for someone who is ill and known to members of the Patrol, for your parents and friends, for those in need. Talk with a leader at your place of worship who is able to help you compile your own prayers and encourage other members of the Patrol to lead prayers, too.

Ask each Scout to make a list of the people he feels the Patrol should pray for. Discuss the lists together – and then ask two members of the Patrol to go somewhere quiet and prepare short prayers for the end of the meeting.

**Hunger**
Discuss with the Patrol what they consider would be the minimum amount of food that they think they need to keep alive. Find out the sort of food that people in Third World countries have to live on – and compare this with your diet. Suggest that one meal at a camp might consist of the sort of food that people in another country have to exist on . . . and send the money you save to a charity concerned to help people who are starving.

**Those in need**
There are many organisations working for those in need, both in this country and overseas. Is one of these supported by your Scout Group or by those who attend your place of worship? If so, find out more about how people are helped. The organisation may be prepared to send a speaker or to loan you a film or video to show at a Patrol meeting. What can your Patrol do to help?

**Scout Law**
At a Patrol meeting give pairs of Scouts a copy of a recent daily newspaper. Ask them to read through the newspaper to find stories that illustrate something in the Scout Law – either carrying out one of the Laws or otherwise.

Chapter 9

# Camps and expeditions

Camping is an enjoyable activity in itself and it also helps Scouts to try a wider range of activities than might otherwise be possible – at a reasonable cost. Learning to camp well means that we can use our camping skills at weekends and for longer periods away from our home area – with the camp site as the base for the things we want to try – without having to pay expensive accommodation fees.

At camp we are away from the pressures of school, homework, jobs and so on, and we have the time to relax and enjoy our Scouting.

In this chapter we are not going to deal with the practical skills involved in camping which are covered in publications such as *Scout Camping* and *Enjoy Camping* (both published by The Scout Association and details will be found in the reference pages at the back of this book). Here we will be looking at planning for camps and expeditions and in particular at the part played by Scout Leaders and Patrol Leaders.

At times all the Patrols in the Troop will be in camp together and at other times the Patrols will camp alone. On other occasions groups of Scouts will camp together – on a training course or because they want to take part in a particular activity.

In the Scout Troop the aim is for the Patrols to camp as units – self-supporting and largely independent of each other. This will be obvious when a Patrol goes off alone on a Patrol camp, but it is just as important for the Patrols to camp as separate units when the Troop is together.

A Patrol is a group of friends and camping brings them together for a few days to work as a team and to enjoy activities. Members of the Patrol are working with each other throughout the year, but in camp they put their training into practice, learn by their mistakes together, achieve success and cope with disappointments. For this reason Scouts should remain in their own Patrols at camp. Don't move a Scout into another Patrol to even up the numbers for catering or for competitions. Patrols should have their own tent – or group of tents – their own cooking gear, axes, saws and so on. If the Troop does not have sufficient equipment for the Patrols to camp like this, it should be a priority to raise money to buy the gear (and in the meantime, the Troop should borrow or hire).

Avoid forming 'camp Patrols' with everyone mixed up in different Patrols from those at home. Camp is the chance for people who have worked together for a few hours each week to experience each other's company for a longer time. It's a test of all the training at Patrol and Troop Meetings throughout the rest of the year.

Before a Patrol can camp successfully as a unit, every member needs training for his part:

- **The Patrol Leader** needs to be trained to lead his Patrol in camp.
- **The Assistant Patrol Leader** has to be ready to play his part as the Patrol Leader's assistant at camp.
- **The Scouts** in the Patrol need the

technical skills to enable them to camp in comfort and to find it enjoyable. They need to feel, too, that they have a part to play in what is going on – and are not there just to fetch the water and find the wood for the fire.

• **Younger Scouts** and those who have joined the Troop with little camping experience want to be shown how to camp – and should not be thrown into things to find out for themselves without training or guidance. Care should also be taken to make sure that they are not picked on because of their age or size.

Training for camp needs to be taken in easy stages. Pitchforking a Troop into a week-long summer camp without training at Patrol and Troop Meetings, and without one or two short training camps beforehand, is a sure recipe for trouble. It is unfair on the leaders and it can result in an inexperienced Scout finding himself totally out of his depth – and he could be put off camping (and Scouting) as a result.

What follows is just a suggested training programme for camping, leading up to the major camp or expedition of the year. You may well decide to do things differently. The important point is that you offer training that is progressive, learning the skills at Patrol and Troop activities and then trying them out in camp. In this way Scouts and their leaders gain confidence in their ability to camp well – and find it enjoyable.

## Patrol Leaders' training camps

It is a good idea for the Patrol Leaders in the Troop to camp together during the year. They probably will in any case – on Patrol Leaders' training courses, when they go off to find a site for the main annual camp or take part in adventurous activities.

If the Patrol Leaders are new to leading their Patrols in camp, it's worthwhile holding a short weekend camp in which the Patrol Leaders are together as a Patrol – each taking it in turn to be the Patrol Leader. Break off during the camp to discuss the leadership style of each Patrol Leader, for it is only through constructive criticism that we will develop an ability to lead that gets results.

## Older Scouts' camp

From time to time the older Scouts in the Troop will be away together – in camp or using indoor accommodation or hostels. The purpose of the few days away may be to take part in some adventurous activities, but take any opportunities that occur to improve your skills – in cooking, in camping, in leading the team.

A survival camp or a weekend living in bivouacs you have built for yourselves can be used to learn something new that, in turn, you can pass on to the younger members of the Patrol.

## Younger Scouts' training camps

Cub Scouts and those who have joined from outside the Group need to learn how to camp as Scouts – and the best people to show them are their Patrol Leaders and Assistant Patrol Leaders.

Arrange a weekend away before your first Patrol camp of the year and well in advance of the main Troop camp where the Patrol Leader, Assistant Patrol Leader and those new to camping in the Patrol are together as a unit. The Patrols will be smaller than usual and this means that the Patrol Leader and Assistant Patrol Leader can concentrate on training the Scouts who are with them.

If the Scout Leader or an Assistant Scout Leader can get away for the weekend to help, so much the better. It will give parents confidence at their son's first camp to know that a Scouter is on hand and younger Scouts in particular may feel happier if an adult is around the first time they are away in camp.

A camp like this is a great opportunity for a Patrol Leader to offer training in practical campcraft skills for whichever award a new member of the Patrol is working.

## Patrol camps

If the aim of Scout camping is to get the Patrols working as independent and self-supporting units, then Patrol camps are something that every Troop should plan within its programme. But don't rush into them without ensuring that everyone taking part is trained and that the Patrol Leader and Assistant Patrol Leader are ready to accept the responsibility.

You might start with a short weekend with all the Patrols camping on one site, with the leaders camping separately but near at hand. This will be the time to sort out any problems that may arise.

Later Patrols could go off alone to a camp site where there is a friendly warden on the spot in case help is needed.

When the Patrol Leaders' Council is satisfied with the standards of camping and leadership at a Patrol camp, the Patrol should be encouraged to find its own site and enjoy camping together. Sites on farms are not always easy to find – and they are even more difficult to keep if the farmer or landowner has experienced a bad Scout camp. Whilst the Patrol Leaders' Council should encourage its Patrols to be adventurous in their camping, it must also accept the responsibility for ensuring that camping standards are high and are maintained that way.

Parents may be concerned at the idea of their son camping with a Patrol without adults at hand. A Troop that builds up a good reputation for high standards of Patrol camping will find that the word gets around – and parents of Scouts in the Troop will reassure those whose sons have recently joined. It's all a question of confidence – between Scouters and Patrol Leaders, and with parents, too.

You will find your own way to reassure parents, but don't overlook the possibility of taking one or two parents to visit a camp – not in any formal way, but perhaps by asking them to come with you to take some food over to the camp or just to see how things are going. Parents who see their son enjoying himself in camp will not need further convincing.

## Summer camp

The following notes provide a checklist for planning a main event which, for convenience, we will call the summer camp, but which in

your Troop might take place over the Spring Bank Holiday or at another time which suits your members best.

**Ask the Scouts**

Find out through Patrol-in-Council meetings what your Scouts want to do at camp and their ideas on where the camp might be held. This helps the Patrol Leaders' Council to decide on the theme of the camp and to plan the site hunt.

**Where to go?**

Hill walking requires hills, canoeing needs water, pioneering can be done on dry land, but a steam or river make it more exciting. Think like this and you will soon build up a picture of the kind of camp site you are looking for.

Write to the Estates Department at Headquarters for a copy of *National, County and District Camp Sites* or borrow a copy from your District Commissioner. When you have decided the area of the country where you would like to camp, write to the County Secretary of the Scout County, enclosing a stamped addressed envelope for details of camp sites or the names of people who may be able to help find a site. (If you do not know the address of the County Secretary, send your letter to Headquarters with a request that it is forwarded.)

**Visit the site**

If you have been successful in obtaining the names and addresses of site owners, write or telephone them first to ask if it will be convenient for you to visit. If the area is not too far from your home, a day visit may be possible. If an overnight stop is called for, consider staying at a Scout camp site (camping or in indoor accommodation), a Youth Hostel or a Scout Group's Headquarters.

You may decide to go off without any sites in mind, calling on landowners and farmers to see if they will allow the Troop to camp. Go in uniform, be polite and remember that you are asking someone to help you, so call at reasonable hours and recognise that the person you are visiting is busy and may find it difficult to spare too much time just because you happen to have dropped in.

Visiting a site beforehand can make all the difference to the successful running of the Patrol System in camp and the site hunt should be undertaken by the Patrol Leaders' Council – the Patrol Leaders and the Scout Leader. If others go along (the Assistant Scout Leaders, for example) that's fine, but the Scouters should not find excuses for usurping the Patrol Leaders' responsibility to help look for the summer camp site by going off together and leaving the Patrol Leaders at home.

Don't forget to write a brief note to thank all those who helped you when you were visiting the area on your return home.

**What to look for?**

- Patrol sites: is there space for the Patrols to camp out of ear-shot of each other?
- Headquarters site: will this be accessible for supplies?
- Latrine site: will this be out of view, but within reach of the Patrols?
- Aspect: are you taking full advantage of the best views?
- Shelter: it's best to visit a summer camp site earlier in the year when the weather is at its worst, for hopefully it will have improved by the time your camp arrives. Will the positions you have chosen for the Patrol sites take advantage of the shelter available from wind and rain?
- Wood: is there wood available on site for your fires or will you have to bring it in? Will you be permitted to use fires or are there safety reasons why stoves would be insisted upon?
- Water: is there a tapped water supply?
- Access: can you bring vehicles within a reasonable distance of the site to off-load equipment? If not, is there a tractor you can borrow?
- Bounds: check with the owner.
- Cattle: will you be camping alone or are cattle likely to share the site with you?
- Other campers: will campers other than Scouts be on site at the same time? If other Scout Troops are camping, make contact before you arrive at camp – there may be an opportunity for some joint activities.
- Soil and drainage: does the soil hold the water and are the Patrol sites well drained?
- Timber: is there a supply for gadgets?
- Activities: look at the site's natural features and decide how you can use these for games and activities.

**Off-site**

- Find out about places to visit.

•Take note of local advice, particularly when adventurous activities are being considered. The local District Commissioner will help you with this.
•Supplies: obtain details of any food suppliers you will need.
•Local information: obtain the addresses of the doctor, hospital, garage or coach operators. Where is the nearest place of worship? Buy a local guide book and obtain bus timetables.

**Permission to camp**

Check with your District Commissioner that the site you are planning to use is not within a restricted area. If the camp is for five or more nights, complete the Form PC (Permission to Camp) which is available from your District Commissioner. This should be returned to your District Commissioner with the registration fee. Your District Commissioner will send the form to the County Secretary of the area in which you will be camping. The Form PC must be received by the County Secretary at least two months before the camp.

**Transport**

Decide how you will travel to and

from the site, how the equipment will be conveyed and if you will need transport on the site.

**Costing the camp**

Prepare estimates of costing well before the camp covering transport, food, camp fees for your use of the site (if any), expeditions and visits, with a contingency amount to cover sundries. Divide this by the numbers camping to work out the cost per person.

**Parents**

Keep parents informed about your plans – giving them the dates of the camp as early as possible in the year to avoid clashing with family holidays. When the District Commissioner and Group Scout Leader have agreed to the camp, send home Permission to Camp Forms on which the parents of Scouts sign to say that they agree to their sons going to the camp. Arrange an evening for parents about six weeks before the camp. Show photographs of the site, collect final camp fees, give the parents a note of the postal address of the camp, the name of an adult in your home area who will have telephone contact with the Troop while they are away and times of departure and return.

**The programme**

Draw up a programme of activities for each day of the camp at a meeting of the Patrol Leaders' Council. An early draft will mean that one or two Patrol Leaders or other older Scouts can start work on the menu and food quantity lists. As activities and expeditions are confirmed and finalised, a more detailed programme can be produced.

## Springboard!

The great thing about a standing camp of the kind we have discussed so far is that it provides a springboard for more adventurous camping. A standing camp is one where a Patrol sets up its tentage, kitchen etc., and remains on the same site for the duration of the camp – using it as a base for activities. Its training value in learning camping skills cannot be overestimated. When a Scout has shown that he can look after himself at a standing camp, he can use the skills he has gained to enjoy different types of camps and a wider range of activities.

The Patrol Leaders' Council has a responsibility to ensure that basic camping skills are learned in camp before Scouts go off on expeditions. Different techniques are needed for lightweight camping, but unless a Scout has the basic camping skills he will not find it easy to adapt. We owe it to the Scout to ensure that he is soundly trained; we owe it to his parents to make sure that he is capable of looking after himself in camp; and we owe it to the good name of Scouting, for the public (in general) and landowners (in particular) expect Scouts to know how to camp and to respect the property of others. A lot of goodwill has been lost over the years when a few untrained Scouts have camped badly. A landowner may have had a succession of camps on his land, but one bad Patrol camp can make him decide never to allow Scouts on his property again. Good camp sites are hard enough to find and it is sad when one is lost to other Scouts simply through lack of training.

## Expeditions

Expeditions can be as basic as a day's hike, cooking your food along the way, or as adventurous as a week-long lightweight hike camp.

Sometimes a Patrol may go off on an expedition, but at other times it might be a group of Scouts who join up because they have a common interest or the Troop may decide to mount an expedition for everyone. You might hike or cycle, go canoeing or sail over a length of river. Youth Hostelling is worth considering, for overnight accommodation is reasonably priced, you can cook your own food and you don't have to carry your camping gear with you.

If you haven't tried expeditions before, there are new skills to learn. Members of the Venture Scout Unit may be able to offer training and some of the Unit might join you on your first expedition. Other organisations – school groups, clubs and so on – may have training courses you could take part in and allow you to borrow their lightweight equipment if the Scout Group does not have its own.

## Other camps

Other camps that members of the Troop might take part in could include:

- **Camps arranged within the Scout Group.** Father and son camps (where Scouts bring their fathers to camp with them for a night or two); mum and son camps (where mothers camp with their Scout sons); family camps (where the whole family comes to camp with the Troop); and Group camps (with the Pack, Troop and Unit camping for a night or so on the same site, sharing some activities together, but having their own programme for part of the time).

- **Camps arranged within the District and County.** Patrol Leaders' training camps; training camps for Proficiency Badges and specialist activities; District and County camps (where Troops get together to meet and to enjoy a wider range of activities); international camps (where Patrols and Troops are joined by Scouts from overseas).
- **Camps arranged by other organisations.** In some areas there are camps for those taking part in the Duke of Edinburgh's Award Scheme; schools, local education authorities and specialist groups often arrange camps for particular activites which may interest some.
- **Camps arranged by the Association nationally.** There are training courses at the Association's National Scout Camp Sites and Activity Centres, and opportunities from time to time for Scouts to camp and meet others from a wider area of the country. Details will be found in SCOUTING Magazine.

Whilst most of the camping that a Scout does will be within his Patrol and Troop, it's good to take advantage of other opportunities from time to time to meet new people and to widen experience.

## Overseas

If members of the Troop take part in an international camp in this country, they will make friends with Scouts from overseas – and want to have an exchange visit. Scouts who are abroad with their parents on a family holiday might meet up with Scouts – and suggest that the Troop camps overseas as a result. One or two older members of the Troop might take part in an overseas camp organised by Headquarters – and enjoy being abroad so much that they want the rest of the Troop to try it. Before you know where you are, the Patrol Leaders' Council will have a summer camp abroad on its agenda.

Advice on taking Patrols or the Troop abroad will be available from your Assistant County Commissioner (International) and from other Scouters and Patrol Leaders who have recent experience. Seek as much advice as you can before jumping in with both feet – for other leaders will be able to offer useful information from which you can start to work.

A site hunt for the Patrol Leaders and Scout Leader does not have to be any more expensive than if you travelled from one end of the United Kingdom to another – and stayed in your home country. You just need to plan your visit carefully and do a lot of research before you go. Help might be at hand from amongst the parents of your Scouts, who may have friends in the country you want to visit or who go there on business and can start making enquiries for you.

Some sites overseas are like our own permanent camp sites in the United Kingdom – where you take your own equipment and use the facilities of a shop, latrines and so on. Other sites offer equipment for hire, whilst in other places there are Scout-owned hostels and centres.

Before you go too far in planning a camp overseas, consult your Assistant County Commissioner (International). He will have contacts to help you, who will not only be able to talk from practical experience, but who will also save you a lot of unnecessary enquiries.

Action 8

# In camp

Camp is the opportunity to put into action the skills that have been learned during the weekly meetings throughout the year. Don't spend valuable time in camp learning the things that could have been tackled at the weekly meeting back home (for example, learn conventional signs and practise using the knowledge in activities in your home area, but in camp go out on a hike or try an expedition to use the skill in an exciting way; sitting outside the tent and learning the conventional signs from scratch is a sad waste of good camping time).

In these *Action* pages we are outlining some activities for weekend or longer camps.

*Bake cakes in a camp oven. Dig a trench fire with a chimney at one end for draught. Use an oil drum or biscuit tin for the oven and insulate it well with thick mud.*

## Activities galore!

An A to Z of just a few activities for the Patrol Leaders' Council to consider when planning their camps.

**Axemanship:** tree felling and clearing wood; logging up timber for the landowner (always ask permission before felling timber).

**Aircraft recognition:** of planes passing overhead or on a nearby airfield.

**Backwoods camping:** spend 24 hours in camp in backwoods-style, building shelters, making your own cooking utensils.

**Backwoods cooking:** try one meal backwoods-style cooked in foil; experiment with planked fish.

**Ballista contest:** Patrols build their own ballistas and see which contraption fires over the longest distance.

**Bird watching:** construct hides and observe bird life. Use a camera to take photographs.

**Cooking:** cook a meal from an overseas country. Run an inter-Patrol cooking competition, giving each Patrol the money to buy the food, so that they plan the menu and decide food quantities. Bake your own bread and cakes.

**Crazy gadget competition:** challenge the Patrols to build the craziest burglar alarm for their food store tent, a camp fire extinguisher, an egg timer – using anything they can find in camp or natural materials only.

**Cycling:** try to take sufficient bicycles to summer camp for each Patrol to have one cycling activity – a local knowledge quiz, an orienteering exercise, a scavenge hunt or just a ride in the countryside.

**Emergencies:** set up a series of emergencies that might occur in camp and let the Patrols show how they would deal with them (a dixie full of water falling from the fire and scalding the cook, a hike tent catching fire, a Scout falling from a tree etc.).

**Estimation:** prepare a list for each Patrol to estimate distance, height, width and weight of things within a mile of the camp site.

**Expedition:** divide the older Scouts into groups for a 36-hour expedition from camp. Set the first group an objective (to reach a specified point by a certain time) whilst the other groups (unknown to the first) trail and report on where the first group went and what they did.

**Experiment:** with the burning qualities of different timbers.

**Fires:** build different types of wood fires and test the efficiency of each by boiling water.

**Games:** try something new (basketball, quoits, croquet, mini-golf, rounders).

**Haybox:** each Patrol makes a haybox before camp, using it to keep soup warm for their return from a night hike or to cook porridge overnight.

*Experiment with different types of wood fire – star fire, hunter's fire, trench fire, gypsy fire, crane fire, bridge fire, reflector fire.*

**Horse riding:** at a riding or pony trekking centre.

**Kite flying:** make your own from natural materials (with a length of string supplied).

**Observation hunt:** give the younger Scouts an activity on their own with a list of questions (how many bars on the gate leading into the parish church, what trees are on the village green etc.).

**Local history:** visit the oldest building and meet the oldest person in the locality.

**Music:** encourage Scouts to bring musical instruments they can play to camp fires; hang mugs, bottles (with varying amounts of water inside) and cutlery on strings – and make your own music.

**Mapping:** make a scale plan of the camp site or a sketch map of the nearest village.

**Open day:** for parents, friends and the local community.

**Patrol Leaders' day 'in charge':** the Patrol Leaders and Scouters/other adults swap over for the day.

**Photography:** give each Patrol a roll of colour print film to take pictures during the camp, using a camera belonging to one of the Scouts in the Patrol. Put the pictures on show at an Open Evening after camp.

**Pioneering:** before camp the Patrols design a pioneering project they wish to build, taking advantage of the camp site's natural features (stream, ditches, woodland).

**Rafting:** remember the safety precautions and ask permission before using rivers or lakes.

**Ropework:** make swings and rope ladders and leave them up for Scouts to use during the camp, checking each day that the knots and lashings are still safe.
**Service:** many of our camps rely on the generosity of landowners who allow us to use their fields, so perhaps the best form of service is to show consideration to our host, ensuring that nothing we do will upset the smooth running of his farm or his

*If you are camping on or near a farm, ask the owner beforehand if a few Scouts who are interested can spend half a day with him.*

business. Offer to tackle a service project – clearing ditches, repairing banks, filling in ruts in tracks, thinning undergrowth in woodlands.
**Sketching:** bring pencils, felt pens, charcoal, watercolours, paper and home-made drawing boards for those who wish to try sketching or painting during spare time in camp.
**Survival:** try a Patrol survival exercise from 6 p.m. in the evening until 10 a.m. the following morning. Give each Patrol their survival kit of oranges, eggs, potatoes, fresh water, flour, two matches and some firewood. Rope off an area in woodland for each Patrol – and they must not come outside that area for the duration of the exercise. They take sleeping bags, groundsheets, night-wear and toothbrushes, build shelters . . . and survive!
**Telephone:** Patrols devise their own intercom systems at home and try them out in camp.
**Tree platforms:** build and (if safe) sleep on them.
**Weather:** keep a weather log.
**Wet days:** prepare some activities in case you have a number of days of continuous rain (compose a camp song, try codes and ciphers, splicing, leaf prints, brass rubbing, whittling, produce a camp newspaper or darn your socks).
**Wood pile contest:** if the Patrols' wood piles are getting low, have a contest to find the Patrol that collects the most dead wood for their pile and chops and stacks it correctly.

## In spare time

There are times at camp when two or three Scouts – or individuals – will enjoy trying a new skill or activity, whilst the rest of the Patrol members are engaged in cooking or some other part of camp life. Here are two ways to cater for this.

## Skill-o-rama

Hand each Patrol Leader a list of things for Scouts in the Patrol to try out during spare time in camp. Some could be tackled by two or three, others by individuals. As the items are completed, a Scouter checks them off on the Patrol's list. Each item can be tackled more than once and by different Scouts. Produce your own list of things to do – here are some to start you off:

- **Bake** three camp biscuits.
- **Draw** a camp cartoon.
- **Cook** an egg in a grapefruit skin.
- **Carve** something in wood.
- **Make** a 'camp monster' from natural materials.

## Free-time activities

Set up a series of activities around the camp site – each Patrol could be responsible for bringing the equipment for, say, two activities and setting them up during the first couple of days in camp. Here are some ideas:

- **Sweet-making:** have the ingredients, stoves and cooking utensils available.
- **Volleyball:** mark out a court – bookings are made with an Assistant Scout Leader.
- **Fishing:** encourage Scouts to bring their own equipment to camp and those without can improvise from materials which you take with you.
- **Garden canes and rubber bands:** have a supply available for Scouts to try out their own mini-pioneering projects.
- **Make a compass:** from half a lemon, a strip of copper and one of zinc, a thin piece of copper wire and a bowl of water (it's known as the Austrian Lemon Compass).
- **Camp cook-in:** have the ingredients available for Scouts to poach an egg in half an orange, cook a sausage in a banana skin, boil water in a paper bag (and up a tree), cook an egg in a hollowed-out potato and to make a reflector fire with foil and bake some cakes.

## Raft regatta

If there is safe water at hand, each Patrol constructs a raft and has time to try it out before the Troop regatta begins.

The normal bathing rules apply during rafting activities and qualified life-savers should be on the bank whilst Scouts are rafting.

Try different methods of buoyancy – oil drums, plastic and polythene containers.

*Raft races – with Scouts using paddles and others swimming alongside to help propel the raft.*

*Two Patrols at a time attempt to land 'bombs' on their opponent's raft ('bombs' are paper bags containing flour).*

*Raft boarding – all the rafts are out at the same time, each one armed with a heaving line, weighted at one end with a bundle of old cloth. The object is to touch the deck of another Patrol's raft with the bundle of cloth. Score number of 'hits'.*

# Incident course

A series of 'incidents' are arranged around the camp site. Each Patrol takes it in turn to attempt each challenge within a set time limit. Some 'incidents' will need more preparation than others – the Patrols could each prepare one of them (and try it out beforehand to make sure it works!). Devise a scoring system that takes into account the time taken at each 'incident' and the success (or otherwise) of the Patrol in tackling the problem.

*The Scout transporter is a method of crossing a stream by means of swinging sheerlegs. Have spars and ropes ready for the Patrol to construct the transporter and time them in this, and in crossing the stream or ditch.*

*The 'electric fence' (fruit netting stretched between two trees or posts) must be crossed by the Patrol and anyone touching it is 'electrified'. Have a selection of spars and ropes on hand for the Patrols to devise their own method of getting over the fence.*

*The Patrols are given a plank of wood, five oil drums or barrels and two long poles. Two Scouts balance on the plank, whilst another moves the barrel at the back to the front. Find the Patrol's best time over a 10m (30ft) course.*

*The Patrol is timed over a 10m (30ft) course. Two stand on the plank and two move the barrels. All are blindfolded with the exception of the Assistant Patrol Leader.*

# Commandos!

Take advantage of whatever is available on your camp site – trees, ditches, slopes in the ground – and devise a commando course on the lines of the one illustrated on page 105.

Early in the camp the Patrols can construct the various items you decide to include and then have a series of events when Scouts are timed over the course.

In the course we have shown, the Scouts start by pushing an old bicycle up a slope. Lifting tackle is fitted to a snatch block on a rope and the bicycle and Scouts have to go across on this to avoid the infested swamp below. The stilts can be made with broomsticks with blocks of wood lashed at one end. The oil drums and plank are needed to cross yet another infested swamp.

START

# Wide games

Wide games are played over ground with plenty of cover and to be enjoyed they need to be a test of stealth and ingenuity, and not of physical strength. A wide game is not an excuse for a punch-up. The simplest wide games require Scouts to break through a cordon, forfeit their 'lives' or prevent the opposing team from getting through to their base.

Most good wide games require the following:

•**A base:** this could be a central base or one for each team. A base needs to be clearly marked, with an adult leader at hand.

•**Quiet!:** games should be as silent as possible and no torches should be allowed – if the game starts before dusk, eyes will soon become accustomed to the gloom.

•**Signals:** a simple whistle system is probably best – one blast for 'start' and 'finish', two blasts for 'stand up and listen, something is going wrong', and three blasts for 'emergency – all return to base'.

•**Teams:** use adult leaders, Venture Scouts and Patrol Leaders to act as the opposition. The Scout teams should compete against the leaders and not against each other. In this way they have to co-operate against the leaders – and Scouts do not get into fights with each other.

•**Stealth:** there should be the minimum of physical contact, thereby encouraging stealth rather than brute force.

•**Lives:** if people are caught, they should be taken to the base and remain there for, say, two minutes and then allowed to rejoin the game. It's no fun if you are caught in the first five minutes and have to stay at the base for the rest of the evening! If 'lives' are involved, use wool tied around the wrist: when a life is broken, a new piece of wool is available at the base – and the Scout joins in the game again.

•**Storyline:** a good storyline adds some excitement to the game, but make sure it does not confuse rather than assist with the fun.

•**Scoring system:** a simple and foolproof system of scoring is essential.

## Game outlines

Here are outlines of some wide games – add storyline to taste!

**Water transfer**

Two or more teams, working from bases near a stream or other water supply, use mugs to transfer as much water as possible from their bases to five buckets hidden over a large area patrolled by guards. On being spotted and named, the Scout tips out any water he is carrying and has to stand or walk with the guard for two minutes.

**Spying**
The teams compete to write down as many details as possible of the enemies' defences, which take the form of all sorts of objects hung in trees. The 'Spy Chiefs' don't just want to know that there is a washing-up liquid bottle or a cotton reel – but what colour it is, what is written on it, when it was bought and details of previous owners – in fact, everything about the objects. The area is heavily guarded and any Scouts who have their lives broken remain in a compound for two minutes before rejoining the game.

**Underground connection**
Two groups of resistance workers in neighbouring, occupied countries are trying to connect together their respective radio sets by joining sisal wire dropped in bundles over both countries by a neutral power. The frontier is clearly marked and has regular patrols up and down it. If a guard finds any wire, he takes a 5ft sample back to base. The two groups must lay the wire as far as possible and ultimately join the two radios.

## Water sports

This is suitable for a warm afternoon by a lake, pond, river or other safe swimming area. Take adequate safety precautions and encourage Patrol Leaders to let non-swimmers try some of the events that do not require swimming ability – provided that they are staged in shallow water where the Scouts can stand up.

Events could include:

- **Nail driving:** one Scout from each Patrol wades into the water with a block of wood, a hammer and some nails. They attempt to drive a nail into the wood under water.

- **Up and under:** Patrols stand in water up to waist level of the shortest Scout in relay formation. The Patrol Leader passes a ball over his head to the Scout behind, who passes it under his legs to the next Scout and so on . . .
- **Kick ball:** relay formation again. Each Scout swims in turn round a marker and back to his Patrol. Legs are used for propulsion, while hands clasp a large plastic ball.
- **Guard the flame:** this is an exciting knock-out contest between pairs of Patrols. Each Patrol has a lighted candle and a supply of washing-up liquid canisters. The Patrol protects its own candle from attack and attempts to extinguish the other Patrol's candle. No splashing!
- **Dressing race:** run as a Patrol race with Scouts dressed in shorts and shirts over trunks. They remove shorts and shirts as they tread water at a marker and swim back to the starting point, carrying their discarded clothing.

Chapter 10

# Where next?

At the beginning of this book we said that the Patrol and Troop do not exist by themselves, but are part of something bigger – the Scout Group, District and County, and Scouting nationally and throughout the world. But we should not overlook the fact that Scouting is much more than that, for it is part of the wider community in which we live – locally, nationally and worldwide.

Throughout a Scout's time in the Troop we should avoid looking inwards to the Patrol and the Troop, assuming that the activities and experiences we offer in Scouting are sufficient for his physical, mental and spiritual growth and development. They are not, but they certainly complement the experiences of family life, of school and work, in clubs and societies to which the Scout belongs, and amongst members of his religious faith.

Our enthusiasm for Scouting should not blind us to the fact that our aim is to help our Scouts to take a constructive place in society. We hope that our Scouts will stay in the Troop until the time comes for them to move into Venture Scouting and that they will find more challenging training activities there. Later they may decide to work as leaders in the Movement or to help Scouting in some other way. But we should not necessarily be disappointed if it doesn't work out like that for every Scout who comes into the Troop.

We are offering a training programme in the Patrol and Troop that will help to widen a Scout's horizons and to show him ways in which he can contribute to society. He may decide that he wants to be of service to others through Venture Scouting or, later, by working in the Movement as an adult. On the other hand, we may have introduced him to a new pursuit or sport and if he decides that he wishes to take that up more seriously by joining a specialist organisation catering for this, we should not be disappointed and think that Scouting has failed in some way. It might be quite the reverse, for we may have opened doors to a life-long interest in an absorbing hobby or sport.

Many other groups of people serve their community in addition to the Scout Movement. Our service projects can open new possibilities for a Scout who wants to be involved – working with young children or the handicapped, taking part in conservation projects or helping the elderly. If a Scout decides that he wants to join a local group working in this way, and that he will not have time for Scouting as a result, we should offer encouragement and continued friendship, rather than imply by any of our actions that he is letting Scouting down.

It is only when a Scout leaves through boredom or frustration that we have failed.

## Moving away

From time to time Scouts and leaders will have to leave the Troop because their families move home or school or work mean that they have to live in another part of the country or overseas. It is important that Members of the Association know that moving away does not mean that they have to lose touch with

Scouting. More than that, the transfer system operated by the Association is there not only to help the Scout who is moving to make contact with Scouting in his new area, but also to give the Scouts in that place advance warning that he is coming so that they can welcome him as soon after his arrival as possible.

The transfer system operates very simply. The Group Scout Leader completes a *Transfer Card* (which is available from your District Secretary) or a similar form which is printed in the *Scout Record Book*. The Group Scout Leader forwards this to the District Commissioner of the District into which the Scout is moving. If the address of the District Commissioner concerned is not known, the *Transfer Card* should be forwarded to the Association's Headquarters – and this is always so with *Transfer Cards* for Scouts who are going to live abroad.

## Venture Scouting

There is no formal Link Badge between the Scout Troop and the Venture Scout Unit – but there are many links that should be developed and that will help an older Scout to move into Venture Scouting.

The requirements of the Explorer Award and the Chief Scout's Award have been designed to bring older Scouts and Venture Scouts together for activities.

The Venture Scout Membership Badge requires a new member to take part in an activity with Venture Scouts and there are many opportunities for Scouts (and particularly older Scouts) to enjoy activities in the Troop in which Venture Scouts are involved – all of which will help to make the move to the Unit less forbidding, for a Scout will be moving into something where he already has friends.

Here are some ways in which links between the Troop and the Unit can be developed:

- **Arrange** joint meetings of the Patrol Leaders' Council and the Unit Executive Committee – leading to more activities together.
- **Invite** members of the Unit to help as instructors in the Troop for specialist subjects.
- **Ask** the Unit to arrange a Patrol or Troop activity – a night hike, a pioneering day, some canoeing or sailing.
- **Try** to have one separate activity for older Scouts in the Troop every so often with the Unit.
- **Build** on the relationship between the Troop and Unit training programmes (which are outlined in the chart on page 50). Scouts working on the Chief Scout's Award should look to the Unit first for expertise and training.
- **Suggest** that one or two Venture Scouts might join you for a weekend training camp, a Patrol Leaders' training course or at the annual camp – as quartermasters or instructors.
- **Plan** activity bases at Troop Meetings, covering training subjects that Venture Scouts could help with.
- **Encourage** Patrol Leaders to invite a Venture Scout to give training in a skill at a Patrol meeting.
- **Keep** the Unit Secretary informed about your activities – and make it clear that the Troop would welcome help from Venture Scouts with training.
- **Make** sure that the Unit Secretary knows the names and addresses of all Scouts in the Troop who are over

fourteen – so that the Unit can take an interest in their progress and invite them to share in some of the Unit's activities. It is far better if the invitation comes direct to the Scout from the Unit, rather than through the Scout Leader.

• **Discuss** Going-up arrangements from Troop to Unit regularly at the Patrol Leaders' Council and at Group Scouters' Meetings.

• **Swap** Scouters – inviting the Venture Scout Leader to run a Troop Meeting (with help from some Venture Scouts), whilst the Scout Leader and his Assistants go to Unit Meetings from time to time (to join in or to sit back and relax for a change).

## The Duke of Edinburgh's Award Scheme

The Duke of Edinburgh's Award Scheme is not a youth organisation, but a programme of practical and adventurous activities – similar in many ways to the programme offered by Scouting. The Scheme emphasises service, expedition work, skills and physical recreation and it can form a further link between the Scout Troop, the Venture Scout Unit and the District Scout Fellowship as it is open to all young people aged from 14 to 25.

The Scout Association is an Operating Authority for the Scheme, side by side with many schools and other youth groups. Some Scouts may already be taking part in the Duke of Edinburgh's Award Scheme at school or through other organisations to which they belong. Advantage should be taken of opportunities for training that are offered through other organisations, whilst at the same time young people from outside Scouting could join in some of the training you offer in the Troop which covers requirements of the Scheme.

There are three Awards – the Bronze Award for those over 14, the Silver Award for those over 15 and the Gold Award for those over 16. The upper age limit for all the Awards is 25. Subject to the age requirements, young people may enter the Award Scheme at whichever level is the best suited to them. If your Troop has not been involved in the Duke of Edinburgh's Award Scheme, the first step is to contact your County Adviser for the Scheme, who will be able to help with literature and tell you where *Record Books* for those taking part may be obtained.

## Scouting is . . .

We have enjoyed preparing this book, but are conscious of the fact that every Scout Patrol and Troop will be different. We have tried to provide suggestions, rather than hard and fast rules, for we appreciate that leaders will learn from their own experiences and from that of others how best to achieve the Aim of the Association which were set out in Chapter 1.

Above all, Scouting is friendliness. It is an adventure and one to be enjoyed every day.

Scouting is to be found in laughter and in a deeper seriousness. It is the contribution of the outdoor life to the art of living. It is a desire to serve others and to grow in courage.

It is a constant apprehension that we are all the children of God.

## Action 9

Some of the activities that follow are for the Patrol or Troop, whilst others might best be tackled by a group of Scouts – perhaps older Scouts – who are working together for part of the Scout Progressive Training Programme. A number of these activities can be enjoyed jointly with members of the Venture Scout Unit. Some will require the help of experts – within the Group, amongst parents or in local clubs and societies.

# Conservation

**•Plant**

Plant and maintain a small garden at home or at your Scout Headquarters, or plant trees on your local camp site to provide more wind protection.

**•Camp conservation**

Help your local camp site to develop a conservation programme – plant trees, clear litter, protect and feed wildlife.

**•Community**

Look around your local area for waste ground, public shrubberies and gardens that are not being looked after. Find out who owns them and offer your services to plant with trees, grass or shrubs.

**•Conservation corner**

Develop a conservation corner at your Scout Headquarters. On tables, shelves and display boards show specimens and illustrations to make your Troop aware of the need for conservation locally. Make your own posters.

**•Birds**

Build bird boxes and feeding tables and set them up at home or offer them to others for their gardens.

**•Boxes and tubs**

Make window boxes and plant flowers, or plant tubs with trees and shrubs. Give them to pensioners for presents.

**•Streams**

Organise a stream improvement project – clearing the stream of litter (and keeping it that way) and planting on banks to prevent erosion. Find out if you can get involved with a local conservation group in work they are doing.

# Local cookery

Many parts of the country have their own traditional local foods – Forfar Bridies (which are like Cornish Pasties, but instead of pastry they are covered in a fatless dough crust), Soda Bread (baked mainly in Ireland) and Cumberland Rum Butter (which was first made in the Port of Whitehaven where ships docked from the West Indies carrying rum).

Find out what the local traditional dishes are in your area. Check the library and ask people who have lived in the place for some time. Try out the recipe – and if it's cakes, bread or biscuits, sell some at your next bazaar.

# Service

Here is an **A to Z of community action** to spark off ideas . . .

**Access.** Prepare a list of buildings and amenities which can be used by the handicapped.

**Broadcasting.** Find out about your local hospital radio station and offer help. In many areas talking newspapers are tape recorded for the blind – can you help in some way?

**Cooking.** Offer to cook a meal for someone who lives alone.

**Decoration.** Paint your Scout Headquarters, local hall or the home of an elderly or handicapped person.

**Eyesores.** Turn waste ground into a garden or shrubbery.

**Fishing.** Take children or the handicapped out for a day.

**Graffiti.** Offer to cover up a wall used by graffiti-writers with a mural.

**Holidays.** Take children who rarely get away from home to a weekend camp.

**Invalids.** Call and offer to do shopping for someone who is ill.

**Invite.** Ask someone you know at school or in your home area who is at a loose end to come to a Troop Meeting – to see if he would like to join.

**Jars.** Collect up bottles and jars and take them to a bottle bank.

**Kites.** Make kites and show young children how to fly them.

**Life-saving.** Learn to life-save and teach others. Train as a life-guard or for mountain rescue later on.

**Mechanics.** Help with maintenance of the Group's minibus or a handicapped person's wheelchair.

**Nettles.** Do rough work for someone who cannot look after their own garden.

**Originality.** Look around you for something original to do to help others.

**Playschemes.** Organise activities for children during the school holidays at your local camp site or around your Scout Headquarters.

**Probation service.** Find out if there is an Intermediate Treatment (or similar scheme) operating locally. The Scout Leader might meet with the leaders of such a scheme to discuss ways in which the Troop would help.

**Qualification.** Train in first aid, rescue, home nursing or some other community work.

**Restoration.** Help a group restoring an historic building.

**Skill.** Teach someone else to play a musical instrument, a new sport or a practical craft.

**Tandem.** Help a Cub Scout or other youngster

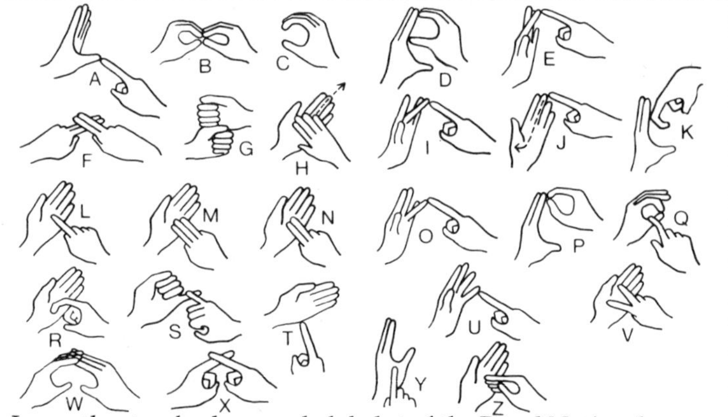


*Learn the standard manual alphabet of the Royal National Institute for the Deaf and use it to communicate with someone who cannot hear.*

to ride his cycle safely and to do simple repairs.

**Urgent.** Ask people you know (at your place of worship, the local school, community centre, etc.) if someone needs your help.

**Vegetables.** Grow vegetables and give them to pensioners.

**Words.** Offer to help produce or distribute the magazine or newsletter published by your Scout Group or by others in your community.

**X.** We are stuck, but visit the lonely, offer to entertain in homes for the elderly and make up parcels of food for those in need.

**Youth involvement.** Find out about any local youth committees. Invite a member to talk to a group of Scouts. Can you help in what they are trying to achieve?

**Zero hour.** Don't wait until someone asks you to help – it's zero hour now!

## Local crafts

Some suggestions for finding out about local crafts – in your home area, when you are away on holiday or in camp . . .

**Bagpipes.** Different kinds are found in Scotland, Ireland and the North East of England. What other localised instruments can you find? Learn to play?

**Campanology.** Find the nearest church with its own bell-ringers and watch them practice. Is there a group of handbell ringers you could join?

**Fashions.** They come and go, but how did people dress in your area 100, 200 or 300 years ago?

**Gates and stiles.** 'Collect' examples of the many different varieties by making sketches or taking photographs.

**Jewellery.** This can be made at home, using stones found locally and on beaches. Do you know someone with a stone polishing machine?

**Knotting.** Decorative knotting was widely practiced by seamen in the days of sailing ships. Find a Venture Scout or other adult who is skilful at knotting and work from there.

**Numismatics.** Coin-collecting is interesting – if you travel abroad on holiday or if you have a link with a Scout Troop overseas. You can exchange not only sets of coins, but postcards of your town, football programmes, comics and so on.

**Onomatology.** This is the study of names and their history. How did the place where you live get its name? How did your own name originate?

**Pottery.** You may have tried this at school. Finding a kiln is sometimes a problem, but see if there are evening classes you might join.

**Thatching.** This is still

common in some parts of the country. Watch a thatcher at work.

**Upholstery.** Find someone locally who does this as a hobby. Repairing furniture and re-upholstering could be a profitable fund raising activity – look out for suitable items at the next jumble sale.

If none of these appeal, ask around your neighbours and friends to find out their hobbies. Spend an hour or so watching – and a new interest may be sparked off as a result.

# Backwoodsmanship

Practise the skills of backwoodsmanship at Patrol meetings and on Troop Night. Spend an afternoon on the local camp site trying them out – and then have a weekend camp making your own shelters and sleeping in them, and cooking backwoods-style.

*When natural materials are hard to find or you do not have permission to cut long grass and bracken, make a shelter from heavy gauge polythene or canvas. Or try an emergency ground shelter with rocks, mud and turf for the walls. Make a base to sleep on putting the following down in order from the ground up – stones or pebbles; sticks or twigs; leaves or moss; grass, hay or straw; and finally heather, feathers or fur.*

*To make the tree stump shelter, secure branches of dead timber to the tree using burdock stems, creepers and other natural fibres. Construct the lean-to shelter by lashing the ridge pole between two trees or supports. Build your framework on this, interlocking timbers or securing them with natural fibres. Thatch from the bottom upwards, overlaying each layer so that the rain will run off. Do not cut live timber without permission; there is usually enough dead wood around.*

# Backwoods cooking

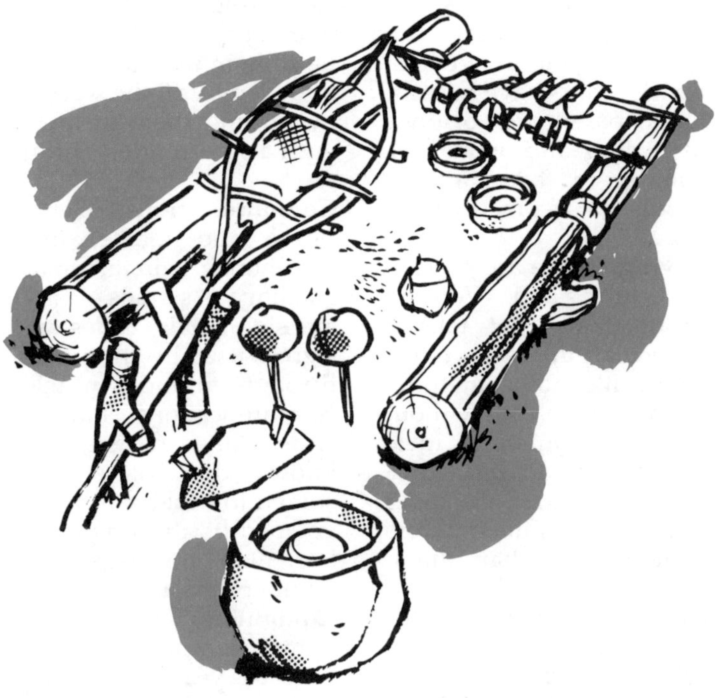

Here's a simple spit fire on which you can skewer meat and vegetables. Make a toasting fork, too. The best woods to use are hazel and ash. Peel the bark and heat the stick to seal the sap. To cook an egg on a spit, bore a small hole at the rounded end and feed in gently a thin, pliable twig, following the contour of the egg. Cook slowly, high above the fire, or the egg will explode.

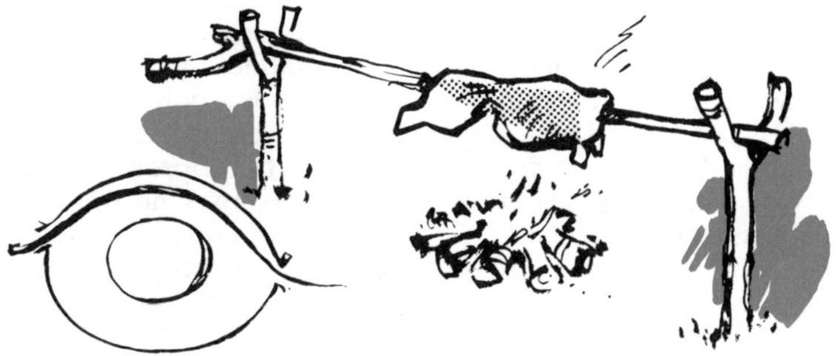

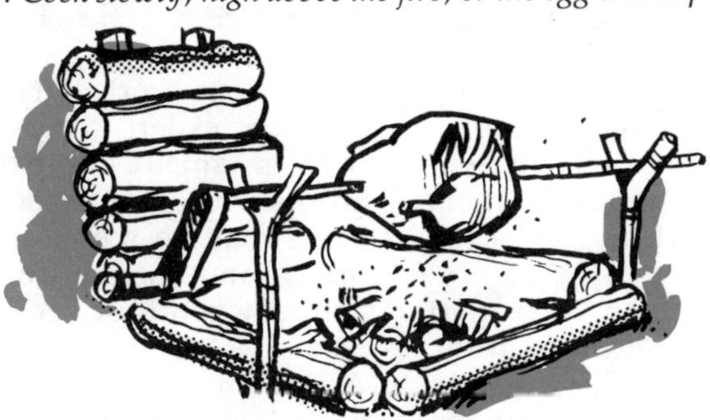

*Try these different methods of backwoods cooking – fish on a greenstick broiler, kebabs on green sticks, eggs in orange skins, apples roasting on twigs and spud egg (with the inside of the potato hollowed out and the egg broken into it). Wait until the fire has burned down to glowing embers before cooking.*

*With a reflector fire, the heat reflects back from the bank of logs onto the meat being spit roasted. Cook jacket potatoes in the embers of the fire. Make a flour and water mixture, roll into small balls and bake camp bread on the logs.*

# Try . . .

The Scout Progressive Award Training Programme and the Proficiency Badge Scheme include a wide range of activities, sports and interests.

Sometimes the Patrol or a few Scouts from different Patrols might be looking for something new to try their hands at. Here are some suggestions, but there are plenty more amongst the awards and badges.

**Amateur radio.** There are a number of amateur radio enthusiasts in Scouting, with an annual Jamboree-on-the-Air each autumn which brings them together throughout the world.

**Angling.** Find an expert and invite all those in the Troop with fishing gear to spend an afternoon together by pond or stream. Team up with a local fishing club.

**Archaeology.** This is not only excavation, but observation and deduction. It is highly skilled and a well-trained expert should be approached to guide Scouts who wish to take an interest in this.

**Archery.** A group of older Scouts might join a local club for instruction and, if interest develops in the Troop, others could take a course of instruction – and archery may become part of the programme during the summer and at camp.

**Art.** Pencil sketching, charcoal drawing, painting, collage work – try to find an expert to work with a small group of Scouts who are interested. Some may be sceptical at first – and then want to join in when they see the results.

**Astronomy.** Another subject where an expert offering training will help, with perhaps two or three Scouts at the most, for the equipment is expensive.

**Athletics.** Interest usually starts at school and develops through clubs, but sometimes Scouting can spot a talent or interest which others have missed. Find a parent who belongs to a club and would be willing to take a few Scouts to a practice session.

**Caving.** There are specialist clubs and Venture Scout Units that take a particular interest in this sport. It's not something to do alone or without training – and an ideal opportunity to link up a small group of older Scouts with trained cavers a little older than themselves.

**Civics.** Find out how this is handled in the local schools – and complement what is offered there. Within your home area there will be councillors, justices of the peace and others who would show a small group of Scouts how things work in your community.

**Collecting.** Find out what your Scouts collect – and help them to enlarge their knowledge of the subject by putting them in touch with a like-minded enthusiast.

**Communications.** Semaphore and morse, field telephones, aircraft marshalling signals and airfield signals, codes and signals used by shipping – through to modern telecommunications. Fun on wide games (if everyone knows the basics) and something that can be developed by those who are keen with the help of an adult enthusiast.

**Computers.** The range of home computers grows year by year (and sometimes week by week!). Encourage those who are interested to work together on projects. They probably do so anyway!

**Drama.** Entertainment is a

traditional part of Scouting – from the camp fire to the Gang Show, from the mime play to the folk concert. Look out for opportunities within the Troop – and also locally (amongst schools, clubs and occasional festivals) and nationally, too (from camp sites running folk weekends to orchestral and folk events organised by The Scout Association).

**Electronics.** Encourage Scouts who are interested to get involved with stage lighting for a Gang Show, with maintaining the installation at your Headquarters – working with adults and learning all the time.

**Fire.** Many Cub Scout Packs visit a fire station, but in the Troop this can be taken a stage further. How safe is your Scout Headquarters in the event of fire? What happens if a tent catches fire at camp or you are called on to help with a fire in woodland? Ask the local fire service if they can help by suggesting a practical training programme for a group of older Scouts.

**First aid.** Encourage older Scouts to take the recognised first aid qualifications of one of the first aid societies – perhaps attending the training with members of the Venture Scout Unit.

**Gymnastics.** Enquire at your nearest sports centre for advice on what courses are available.

**Handicrafts.** Is there someone locally who can help with basket-making, bookbinding, brass-rubbing, clay modelling, joinery, leatherwork, origami, toy making, wood carving . . . ? The list is endless!

**Karting.** Does a Venture Scout Unit in your area have its own karts or is there a club you should visit?

**Meteorology.** Visit a weather station. Keep your own local weather records.

**Mountaineering.** Another case of finding the experts – in the Venture Scout Unit, District or County?

**Photography.** Many families have a camera of some sort – and a local photographer can help to show a group of Scouts how to make the best use of what they have available.

**Road safety.** Are there off-the-road driving training facilities available locally for those in the 15-plus age range?

**Scoutcar races.** Arrange your own – enter for the National Scoutcar Races.

**Skiing.** Where is the nearest dry-ski slope?

**Skin-diving.** Are there Venture Scouts who are trained or is there a club you can link up with?

**Social activities.** Go to the cinema, theatre, disco, debate, concert . . .

**Swimming/lifesaving.** Get trained – and then help train others.

**Vehicle maintenance.** This might start with dad's car and the Scout Group's vehicle.

Look around you. What needs doing? Can you help to create a garden, work with a play group, help at your place of worship, teach others a skill you have learned . . .

# Reference section

## Publications

The following books are available from Scout Shops Limited. The letter 'S' indicates that the book has been written for Scouts and the letter 'L' means that the book has been prepared for Leaders.

**Published by**
**The Scout Association**

*Policy, Organisation and Rules*: details of the Association's structure, method, training programme, awards and safety rules.

*Scout Proficiency Badges*: lists the requirements for all Scout Proficiency Badges, including Airmanship and Seamanship stages.

*The Fun of Scouting* by Peter Browne: the training and activity book covering the Scout Membership Badge, the Scout Award, the Pathfinder Award and the Patrol Activity Award (S).

*Challenge and Adventure* by Derek Capper: the training and activity book covering the Scout Membership Badge, the Explorer Award, the Chief Scout's Award, the Patrol Activity Award, the Leadership Award and the Chief Scout's Challenge (S).

*The Scout Record Book*: for a Scout to record his individual progress in Scouting and containing full details of the training programme (S).

*Scout Camping* by Tony Kemp and Jeremy Sutton-Pratt (L).

*Enjoy Camping* by Doug Mountford: a pictorial guide to Patrol and Troop camping (S).

*The Group Council* (L).

*Scout Games* compiled by Nigel Frankland.

*The Scout Group* by John Deft (L).

*Scouting for Boys* by Robert Baden-Powell – available in a definitive hardback edition (L) and in paperback (S).

*Scout Prayers*.

*Scout Pioneering* by John Sweet.

*Pioneering in Town and Country* by John Sweet.

*The Scout Fire and Folk Song Book* by Peter Brooks, Tony McSweeney and Brian Sims.

*A Dictionary of Knots* by Eric Franklin.

*The SCOUTING Diary* (L).

**Books from other publishers**

*Games Galore* by Colin McKay (Brown, Son and Ferguson).

*The Scout Annual* (World International Publishing) (S).

*The Scout Diary* (Charles Letts) (S).

*Whizz Kids Camping* by Ron Jeffries and Paul Moynihan (Macdonald) (S).

**SCOUTING Reprints**

Material reprinted from SCOUTING Magazine – the following are of particular interest to Scout Leaders and Patrol Leaders:

*Troop Night Programmes*
*More Troop Night Programmes*
*Patrol Leader Training*
*The Patrol System*
*Energise* (ideas for adventurous activities)

**SCOUTING Training Charts**

A list of the range of charts is published regularly in SCOUTING Magazine – these are available on mail order or from Scout Shops Limited.

**The Resource Centre**

The Resource Centre publishes a catalogue of fact sheets and other material available concerned with Scout training.

**Record-keeping**
Scout Shops Limited publish a range of stationery and the like (and details are in their catalogue). Two other companies publishing similar material are: Scoutaids, 77a High Street, MIDSOMER NORTON, Near Bath, Avon; and Scoutink, Stacey and Son Limited, 99 Kingsland High Street, LONDON E8 2PE.

**SCOUTING Magazine**
SCOUTING is the national magazine of The Scout Association and is available from Scout Shops Limited, newsagents or on subscription (details from SCOUTING at Baden-Powell House). In addition to feature articles on all aspects of the Movement, there are regular training supplements of value to Scout Leaders and Patrol Leaders, up to date information on training programmes, details of training and other opportunities for Leaders and Scouts at home and overseas, amendments to *Policy, Organisation and Rules* . . . and much more. Essential reading for every Scout Leader and Patrol Leader.

# Headquarters services

The Association's Headquarters is at three centres:

**Baden-Powell House, Queen's Gate, LONDON SW7 5JS (01-584 7030).** The offices of the Chief Scout and the Chief Executive Commissioner are here, and the following services are provided: administration, archives, development, District Scout Fellowship, finance, Field Commissioners, legal, overseas, publications, public relations, relationships, SCOUTING Magazine, Scouting and Unemployment Programme, Scoutreach.

**Churchill Industrial Estate, LANCING, West Sussex BN15 8UG (0903 755352).** The Head Office of the Association's trading organisation, Scout Shops Limited, is based here and the following services are available: grants, insurance, records (warrants, census, registrations, decorations and awards).

**Gilwell Park, Chingford, LONDON E4 7QW (01-524 5246).** The Programme and Training Department provides advice on the training programme for Cub Scouts, Scouts and Venture Scouts; information on Beavers, Handicapped Scouting, Sea and Air Activities and the Duke of Edinburgh's Award Scheme; advice on leader training and information on activities and national events; and support material through the Resource Centre. The Estates Department is also based here, providing information on National, County and District camp sites and activity centres.

# Addresses

**Scottish Headquarters,** The Scout Association, 18 Hanover Square, EDINBURGH EH2 2QN.

**Northern Ireland Headquarters,** The Scout Association, 4th Floor, 38 Dublin Road, BELFAST BT2 7HN.

**World Scout Bureau,** Case Postale 78, 1211 GENEVA 4, Switzerland.

**Baden-Powell House International Hostel,** Queen's Gate, LONDON SW7 5JS.

**Hawkhirst Adventure Camp,** Plashetts, HEXHAM, Northumberland NE48 1QZ.

**Scottish Scout Activity Centre,** LOCHGOILHEAD, Argyll PA24 8AQ.

# The Scout Troop

## Index